Mobile Messaging and Resourcefulness

This book advocates a new p   approach
to unpacking mobile commu   .... a more informed
understanding of individuals' communicative practices in cities today.
Drawing on data from a group of ordinary working people, multilingual
individuals from superdiverse cities across the United Kingdom, the
volume brings observations from this data together to form a new
concept of 'resourcefulness' as a means of explaining the emergent sense
of agency individuals develop towards remediating existing forms of
technology in their everyday lives. The book in turn establishes the notion
of the 'networked individual' by way of demonstrating the ways in which
communicative practices cross spaces and platforms. Further chapters detail
examples to highlight resourcefulness at work in enabling more efficient
business communication, routes to self-expression and the creation and
development of social support systems, while a concluding chapter looks
at both the limitations and possibilities of resourcefulness and directions
for future research. This innovative volume will be of particular interest to
students and researchers in applied linguistics, sociolinguistics, linguistic
ethnography, and media and communication studies.

Caroline Tagg is Senior Lecturer in Applied Linguistics at The Open
University, UK. Her research into language and digital technologies rests
on the understanding that digital communication practices are deeply
embedded into individuals' wider lives. She is author of *Taking Offence
on Social Media* (with Philip Seargeant and Amy Aisha Brown, 2017)
and *Message and Medium* (with Mel Evans, 2020).

Agnieszka Lyons is Senior Lecturer in Applied Linguistics at Queen
Mary University of London. Her research employs multimodal and
mediated discourse analytic as well as ethnographic approaches to explore
the discursive construction of embodied identity in polycentric migrant
environments. She has published on issues related to migration and mobility
in *Language in Society*, *Journal of Pragmatics* and *Social Semiotics*, among
others.

Routledge Focus on Language and Social Media
Editors: Sirpa Leppänen and Caroline Tagg

Designed for socially oriented researchers with an interest in language and technology, this series covers innovative and in-depth studies of communication through and around social media. The series takes a broad and inclusive approach, which recognises the rapid expansion of the field, due not only to the recent proliferation of social media platforms and the increasing reach of the internet across our working, social and personal lives, but also to broadening interpretations of what both 'language' and 'social media' entail, including growing recognition of the multiple modes used alongside language, and the embedding of social media in our everyday lives. Language and Social Media publishes studies concerned with a wide range of relevant issues and concerns. These include, but are not limited to:

- Identity work; identity trouble
- Constructing and debating belonging, communality, relations and networks
- Sharing, collaboration and participation
- Discourse trajectories and recontextualizations
- Complexity, diversities and differences
- Governance, surveillance and control of/in social media activities and interactions
- Digital literacies and informal learning
- Creativity and play
- Affect and attachment
- Language and social media in commercial and professional practices
- Media/language ideologies
- The wider roles of social media in the lives of individuals, groups and communities.

Language, Gender and Parenthood Online
Negotiating Motherhood in Mumsnet Talk
Jai Mackenzie

https://www.routledge.com/Routledge-Focus-on-Language-and-Social-Media/book-series/LSM

Mobile Messaging and Resourcefulness

A Post-digital Ethnography

Caroline Tagg and Agnieszka Lyons

NEW YORK AND LONDON

First published 2022
by Routledge
605 Third Avenue, New York, NY 10158

and by Routledge
4 Park Square, Milton Park, Abingdon, Oxon, OX14 4RN

Routledge is an imprint of the Taylor & Francis Group, an informa business

© 2022 Caroline Tagg and Agnieszka Lyons

Library of Congress Cataloging-in-Publication Data
A catalog record for this title has been requested

ISBN: 9780367143541 (hbk)
ISBN: 9781032269412 (pbk)
ISBN: 9780429031465 (ebk)

DOI: 10.4324/9780429031465

Typeset in Times New Roman
by Deanta Global Publishing Services, Chennai, India

Contents

Illustrations

Figures

Table

Acknowledgements

We'd like to thank all our participants on the TLANG project, whose mobile messaging practices and generosity with their time made this book possible. Our thanks go also to the project team for their support and insights, particularly Adrian Blackledge, Angela Creese, Rachel Hu, Li Wei and Zhu Hua.

1 Introduction

This book explores how mobile communication – in the form of mobile messages sent via apps like WhatsApp and WeChat – fits into and shapes people's social and working lives. It looks at how mobile messaging *facilitates* carrying out everyday tasks and maintaining relationships with family, friends and colleagues, and the opportunities it provides for self-expression and self-presentation. It also considers the extent to which the new technology *transforms* our lives and what it means to be social – to do, to be and to relate to others – in the early twenty-first century. The book points to the need to recognise ordinary people's agency in navigating and exploiting increasingly complex technological environments, while acknowledging that choices are constrained and enabled by the surrounding practices, discourses, people, technologies and material objects.

Since the turn of the twenty-first century, our lives, relationships and identities have become increasingly dominated by mobile devices, especially internet-enabled mobile phones (or smartphones). Mobile phones not only allow us to carry out conversations with people who are not physically present, but to do so while we are on the move and simultaneously engaged in other activities. Our mobile phone interactions – whether mediated by voice, video or mobile messaging apps – interweave with and mutually support our physical contexts and offline activities, facilitating our journeys, helping curate significant life events, or distracting us from boredom. On the one hand, through our mobile phones, we are constantly available to others regardless of our physical location; but, on the other hand, our attention is divided and we are present simultaneously in different spaces – we can, for example, send sporadic messages to a colleague and post a selfie on Instagram while on a voice call with a friend and helping to prepare a family meal at home. Whether this is perceived positively or negatively, how we present ourselves, how we maintain relationships and how we get things done are shifting in line with our changing use of technologies. For many people, their mobile phone has become an indispensable tool for

DOI: 10.4324/9780429031465-1

maintaining a sense of self, managing relationships, socialising and carrying out professional and personal activities. In other words, mobile phones, along with various social media platforms, messaging apps, emoji and gifs have become part of our communicative repertoires, the set of resources through which we make meaning.

In this book, we work with the concept of the *communicative repertoire* – the range of linguistic and other semiotic resources available to individuals and which people draw upon in communication with others. We are motivated by the key observation that our repertoires have expanded in recent years to include mobile technologies, social media and a whole range of digital resources. We seek to understand the implications of this reconceptualisation of repertoire for individuals, exploring the ways in which their mobile communication intersects with and mutually shapes their offline interactions. We show how people draw *resourcefully* on their mobile phones as part of their wider communicative repertoires, highlighting their human agency in exploiting the available technologies to achieve communicative and social goals, while foregrounding the contextually bound nature of their technology use. In doing so, we show how detailed sociolinguistic understanding of seemingly ordinary, fleeting conversations carried out via mobile phone messaging apps can play a key role in helping us appreciate the nature of individual lives and relationships in contemporary society.

In the rest of this introductory chapter, we explain the research project on which this book is based and introduce the key mobile phone users who feature in the book, before outlining how our study builds on and extends existing understandings of communication mediated by mobile messaging apps.

The Research behind the Book

The book explores the communicative practices of six multilingual individuals living and working in ethnically diverse neighbourhoods in Birmingham and London. Our participants use various communication apps on their mobile phones to carry out business transactions, maintain social support networks and express themselves in the context of their wider working, social and domestic lives. We focus on how mobile messaging exchanges carried out through multiple apps intertwine with everyday face-to-face activities and wider identity projects, strengthening existing relationships, and we point to the role that language and other semiotic resources play in achieving this.

The research in this book is part of a four-year ethnographic project called 'Translation and Translanguaging: Investigating Linguistic and Cultural Transformations in Superdiverse Wards in Four UK Cities' (TLANG) (www.tlang.org.uk) which ran from 2014 to 2018 (see Chapter 2 for more details). The project aimed to understand how people communicate across diverse languages and cultures, and deploy their communicative repertoires across a complex entanglement of face-to-face encounters and online interactions at work, at home and in other social spaces. The TLANG project documents the ways in which people in many ethnically and linguistically diverse urban neighbourhoods draw on partially overlapping communicative repertoires to negotiate difference and sameness in face-to-face and online interactional encounters (Creese and Blackledge 2019; Tagg and Lyons 2018; Zhu Hua et al. 2017; Callaghan et al. 2018). Digital media, and mobile phones in particular, have become increasingly important in the process of newcomers integrating into a new country, from sourcing information to setting up translocal support networks (Gomes 2018; Leurs and Smets 2018). However, as Androutsopoulos and De Fina (2021) note, there has been less scholarly attention on the role of language in digitally enabled mobility, and more empirical research is needed to understand how migrants' dynamic linguistic repertoires intersect with various digital media resources in the course of their everyday lives.

This book puts forward a *post-digital* ethnographic approach which recognises that the digital is no longer a separate or exotic object of enquiry but inherent to the social lives of many people. Our approach offers a holistic understanding of the role of mobile communication in individuals' communicative practices across offline and digitally mediated spaces. In line with TLANG, the book focuses not on university students and young people (who tend to be the focus of attention in sociolinguistics research on mobile messaging) but on people less often included in relevant studies: older, harder-to-reach demographic groups such as ordinary working people living with their families in contemporary city spaces. The six individuals in this book – four women, two men – are multilingual people whose complex lives have been shaped by mobility. All six migrated to the UK and now live and work in one or other of the country's two largest cities: London in the south-east and Birmingham in central England. In describing them as 'ordinary' working people, we recognise the degree to which contemporary societies are marked by mobility – including domestic and temporary migrations – and the extent to which 'commonplace diversity' is experienced as a normal part of life (Wessendorf 2014). Their stories of 'becoming' (Blackledge et al. 2015) feature many of the struggles that migrants face in securing a livelihood in a new and unfamiliar labour market – precarity, financial difficulties, racism. In our research, we witnessed their determination to overcome such challenges and observed them reaching important milestones on their journey: obtaining legal status, setting up businesses, making local contacts, succeeding against the odds.

We also tentatively describe these individuals' use of mobile messaging as 'ordinary' in the sense that it is deeply embedded in their everyday routine practices. They are not, in the main, early adopters of technology or pushing the boundaries of what is technically possible; instead, their mobile interactions would likely resonate with other users in similar contexts, even as they perceive and take advantage of particular affordances for their own local purposes. The fact that our participants are older than those in many studies of mobile messaging is important because the focus on young people risks neglecting the full range of uses made by other groups. This in turn obscures our understanding of the extent to which technologies themselves are shaped by users and their practices. For example, one limitation to much existing work into SMS text messaging and other messaging apps (discussed below and addressed in this book) is the focus on social and personal uses of mobile messaging, despite the wide and increasing range of uses to which mobile messaging can be put (Thurlow and Poff 2013). Similarly, while much research focuses on the way in which online communication encourages playful language mixing among university students and other young people, our findings draw attention to the use of mobile messaging apps to carve out ethnically and linguistically homogenous social support networks in superdiverse cities. Importantly, any focus on young people may draw attention towards innovation and novelty at the expense of the often more conservative and settled practices of older technology users.

Introduction to the Central Characters

Below we introduce the six people that feature in this book. The names are pseudonyms, with the exception of the four Birmingham-based participants, all of whom were consulted at length and agreed to be named. Our understanding of their lives draws on project reports which are openly accessible from the TLANG website (Blackledge et al. 2015, 2016, 2017, 2018; Zhu Hua et al. 2015, 2016).

Edyta and her husband Tadeusz arrived in the UK from Poland in 1997. They originally planned to stay for a few years, save some money and return to Poland, where they had bought a house. Like many other Polish migrants in the UK, the couple eventually decided to stay and used their savings to open several Polish shops. At home, they spoke Polish and had mainly Polish friends. At the time of data collection, they had a 10-year-old daughter Zuzanna, who attended a local Catholic school and a Polish Saturday school. According to her father, Zuzanna preferred to speak English even to her Polish friends and sometimes used English in conversations with her parents when she could not find a word in Polish. Edyta and Tadeusz learnt English mainly after arriving in the UK. Their English at the time of observation, despite limited vocabulary, was functional and they seemed at ease with it. As most Poles of their generation, Edyta and Tadeusz were taught Russian at school. However, Edyta reported that she had forgotten most of her Russian, and Tadeusz said that he only found Russian useful after he moved to the UK. We worked with Edyta between September and December 2014, and we look at her mobile communication across contexts in Chapter 4.

Joanne, who was born and raised in Shenyang, Liaoning Province, China, was an Advice and Advocacy Officer at the Chinese Community Centre Birmingham (CCCB). She studied English Literature for her BA degree and worked as a tour-guide in China after graduation for several years. She was then sent by her company on a one-year language-enhancing course in Scotland, where she met her husband, who was originally from Hong Kong and a Cantonese speaker, working in catering in Scotland. They moved to Birmingham in 1999 and had been living in the city since then. Joanne had been working at the Centre since 2003 in different roles. At the time of data collection, her role involved supporting clients with a range of issues including welfare benefit claims, passport applications, school admissions and council tax. She spoke Cantonese as well as Mandarin and English, translating between the three languages as part of her work. She kept in regular contact with friends and family members in China through WeChat. With the exception of email at work, WeChat was the only digital platform Joanne used on a daily basis. WeChat for her was a space in which different kinds of relationships and communicative functions played out. We worked with Joanne in the summer of 2016 and we explore her business practices in Chapter 3 and her communicative repertoire on WeChat in Chapter 5.

Joe arrived in the UK from Hong Kong aged 14 with his younger brother to attend boarding school, returning to Hong Kong in the school holidays. He took a degree at Southampton University and then worked in Manchester, before going into business as co-owner and manager of a beauty and hair salon in Birmingham, where he lived with his partner. He had taken up volleyball at university, and at the time of data collection he was still playing, as well as coaching the university club. Outside work, he had a social network of close friends who he saw regularly and with whom he used WhatsApp to organise social events and keep in touch. He used both SMS text messaging and WhatsApp extensively to coordinate his working and social lives. In terms of his linguistic repertoire, Joe was a highly proficient English user. Although he could speak Cantonese and members of his family wrote in their WhatsApp group in Cantonese, Joe responded in English and there is no evidence across our dataset to suggest that he ever wrote in a Chinese script; we noted only one instance in which he wrote in Romanised Chinese. We worked with Joe between September 2015 and January 2016, and we discuss his communicative repertoire in Chapter 5.

Kang Chen and his wife Meiyen Chew were a couple with three young children who ran a butcher's stall in the Birmingham Bull Ring indoor market. Kang Chen was originally from Changle in Fujian, in the south of China. He had relatives in the UK, and had arrived in 2001. In 2006, he met Meiyen Chew, who was from Furong in Malaysia, when they were both working in a take-away restaurant in the south of England. Kang Chen talked about his eagerness to travel, which he attributed to the experiences of others who had migrated. Kang Chen described his experience since migrating to the UK as mixed. Despite good financial reasons to live and work abroad, he was uncertain whether 'the stress and struggle' was worth it. He said he could never be as relaxed and comfortable in the UK as when he was in his own country speaking his own language. Both Meiyen and Kang spoke English with employees and customers at work, although proficiency in English was not a requirement for their work and Kang did not always feel comfortable using the language. We worked with Kang Chen between September and December 2014, and we discuss Kang's mobile resourcefulness at work in Chapter 3.

Marta was born in the north-east of Poland, near the Belarussian border. She first came to the UK in 2003 to visit a friend, and decided not to return to Poland. She already had a BA degree in acting from a drama school affiliated to a UK university and had been working towards a diploma in translation in London. At the time of our study, she was in her early 30s and worked as a self-employed artist and artistic director of a non-profit art organisation in East London. Marta also had a portfolio of part-time jobs including 'front of the house' duties at two arts centres, and as translator and interpreter. Her linguistic repertoire included Polish, English and Podlaski Dialect (a dialect of Polish in her hometown), as well as German (studied for four years at school) and Russian (mainly passive knowledge). Marta was an experienced and confident user of technology, and was active via social media in looking for collaborators, building networks and promoting her work. The online persona that Marta presented was that of a performer, artist and someone who crossed linguistic, cultural and artistic boundaries. We worked with Marta between March and July 2015, and we discuss her communicative repertoire and sharing practices in Chapter 5.

Winnie, born in Hong Kong, worked as a customer experience assistant at the Library of Birmingham. In 1995, she migrated to the UK, where she met and married her husband with whom she had two children, both grown-up at the time we worked with her. Having started work at the Library in 2000, Winnie was proud of her job and saw it as an important element of being an independent woman. At the time of data collection, the Library was being restructured and there was a great deal of uncertainty over Winnie's and her colleagues' jobs. A Cantonese speaker, Winnie was also a proficient user of English, although she showed a concern to improve her written English, in part to secure her job prospects. Winnie had a circle of friends with whom she met up regularly, and was in constant and active communication with family members. Winnie was not a prolific user of mobile messaging, and not as confident or innovative in her use as, for example, Marta, but she nonetheless used it proficiently to organise her social and personal life, and to enact various social roles, as parent, parent-in-law, sibling, employee and friend. We worked with Winnie to document these and other practices between March and July 2015, and we look at her mobile communication practices in Chapter 3.

In this book, we focus on these individuals' mobile communication in the form of *mobile messaging* – exchanges carried out through short, text-based multimodal messages sent through mobile messaging apps such as WhatsApp – rather than voice calls or other channels and platforms enabled by the mobile phone. This focus is motivated by our participants' preference: mobile messaging was the technology they predominantly used in their daily communication, and most had less time for and interest in social media sites such as Facebook, Twitter and Instagram. The TLANG project set out to explore what we called 'social media' without preconceptions as to which apps or platforms our participants might be using and what they were doing on them. We found ourselves collecting mobile phone messages rather than any other kind of digital data from participants. We may have played a role in shaping what our participants chose to share with us – for example, we primarily met our participants at work, where they had their phones to hand but not their personal home laptops or tablets. Having said that, all six spent most of their days at work and, in that respect, the data we collected reflects what they spent most of their time doing online. For working adults aged over 30 with busy working and family lives, mobile messaging is a useful tool which fits in around their other commitments, and which could be used on the move to micro-manage parallel and upcoming activities.

Mobile Messaging

Mobile messaging was first introduced to the world in the form of *SMS text messaging*, a short message service added to mobile phones in the 1990s. Intended as a way for phone companies to contact customers, it was quickly embraced by users and had a profound impact on how people communicated and arranged their social lives (Katz and Aakhus 2002). This was before mobile phones were internet-enabled and when they had number keypads and predictive text functions. Among linguists, the focus was on how these technological constraints – together with the communicative demands – shaped the language used (Shortis 2016; Thurlow 2003). Several studies focused on an SMS writing style called 'txt' (Shortis 2007) or txtspk (Crystal 2001), which was found to be characterised by acronyms, abbreviations and homophones (Al-Khatib and Sabbah 2008; Chen and Tan 2013; Chiluwa 2008; Dürscheid and Stark 2011; Fairon and Paumier 2006; Haggan 2007; Härd af Segerstad 2002; Lexander 2011). Text messaging was also found to contain features of orality or involvement including repetition, vague language, speech-like discourse markers and formulaic phrases (Tagg 2012) and, in multilingual contexts, code-switching and bilingual language play (Deumert and Masinyana 2008; Morel et al. 2014). These latter studies focus on user creativity, indicating a move away from the initial exploration of language form (see also Busch 2021; Lyons 2014; Tagg 2013) and towards an interest in the social contexts in which mobile messaging takes place (see also a handful of ethnographic studies such as Lyons 2014, 2018; Spilioti 2011; Tagg 2016; Velghe 2014; Lexander and Androutsopoulos 2021). Such studies begin to show how text messaging is shaped by its users' attitudes, identities and relationships, and by the physical and social contexts in which mobile communication takes place.

   With the advent of smartphones, the early 2000s saw the introduction of a range of internet-enabled messaging apps, including *WhatsApp* (an American app released in 2009 and owned by Facebook, with around 2 billion users worldwide in 2020), *Viber* (a Japanese app popular in

Eastern Europe, Russia, the Middle East and some of Asia, released in 2010) and *WeChat* (a Chinese app released in 2011 and owned by Tencent, with over 1 billion users, mainly based in China). Users may see these apps as more 'conversational' (Church and de Oliveira 2013) and there is some evidence to suggest that WhatsApp users tend to write a series of shorter messages rather than packing everything into one message as in SMS (Dürscheid 2016; König 2019). This may be because internet-enabled apps such as WhatsApp are perceived as being free, while the fact that interactants are notified when a user is online and/or typing heightens the need to respond immediately. These apps tend to offer more functionalities than SMS – including group chats, voice messaging and location sharing. Their advent and growth has been accompanied by developments in technology that shape the user experience and, in turn, the nature of their communication and language practices. One example is the practical one of changes to mobile phone design, including the adoption of a QWERTY keyboard and autocorrect options; another is the growing availability of preconfigured semiotic resources, such as emoji, stickers and GIFs (Albawardi 2018; Al Rashdi 2018; Zhou et al. 2017), as well as the possibility to embed and share web-based resources. Interestingly, although the use of txtspk has declined as the technological constraints have lifted, users continue to draw on a similar range of graphic resources, including respellings (Evans and Tagg 2021), emoticons (Pérez-Sabater 2018) and punctuation (Busch 2021), pointing to the social and communicative functions of these features.

One of the key characteristics of mobile messaging is its relative *privacy* in comparison to public or semi-public internet sites such as online forums or social media sites. Mobile messaging communication tends to take place between individuals or among closed networks. Private contexts such as these have generally received less scholarly attention, not least because of the difficulties in accessing data from one-to-one interactions or closed groups (Androutsopoulos and Juffermans 2014). Therefore, as researchers of language and communication, we likely know less about mobile messaging than we do about online forums or dominant social media sites such as Facebook. Gaining access to such closed contexts can, however, provide key insights into the role that language and technology play in people's personal, social and economic lives. Lyons (2020), for example, explores how new mothers co-construct expertise in a WhatsApp group as they share experiences, challenge medical opinion and arrange face-to-face meetings. Lexander and Androutsopolous (2021) focus on the use of various online apps by multilingual families, using interview, observation and self-selected extracts from digital interactions to explore the intersections between people's language and media choices in their interactions with friends and family. Staehr and Norreby (forthcoming) also take families as their starting point, exploring everyday family encounters which stretch across offline and online spaces. They focus on the embedding of social media in the everyday practices of family socialisation. Our earlier research in the TLANG data shows how migrant micro-entrepreneurs based in the UK use mobile messaging to build and access local and transnational social networks for social and economic support (Tagg and Lyons 2017), through which they negotiate their sense of cultural identity and belonging (Lyons et al. 2019).

Another key characteristic of mobile messaging since the 1990s is the *portability* of mobile devices, which means that mobile messages can be typed, sent, received and read while interactants are on the move. SMS text messages can be contrasted with computer-mediated communication carried out in front of a computer, at home, or at work. The portability of the mobile phone and the fact that individuals tend to keep their phones with them at all times heightens the perceived *intimacy* between interactants, with messages going straight to an individual's pocket. With advances in mobile technology, sites and services once accessed only through a computer have now converged onto the mobile phone (Madianou 2014), and mobile messaging apps are often accessed from the same device as web browsers, social media apps and email. The convergence of various platforms onto the mobile phone increases the fluidity with which people move between online and offline spaces in their daily lives, and the complex ways in which the physical and digital intertwine in the carrying out of everyday social activities, often while interactants are physically on the move (Cohen 2015; Lyons 2020; Lyons and Ounoughi 2020). Despite initial assumptions of an online/offline divide, our research suggests that users often make physical contexts relevant in online settings, through posting photos or sharing location information (Lyons and Ounoughi 2020), as well as their use of deixis (Lyons 2014), all of which may increase involvement in interactions (Tagg and Hu 2017) and heighten feelings of intimacy across distance by providing an immediate window into interactants' physical worlds (Lyons 2014, 2015; Lyons and Ounoughi 2020; Lyons and Tagg 2019). The functionalities of networked digital media – pasting, copying, embedding – make possible this fluid intermingling of contexts which increasingly forms an essential part of many people's digital repertoires 'on the move'. A focus on closed mobile messaging contexts is thus important because, as Androutsopoulos and Juffermans (2014) point out, it enables researchers to explore digital media as embedded in users' everyday lives. How repertoires are deployed in mobile interactions can, from this perspective, only be understood in relation to an individual's wider social networks and identity performances, which extend across offline and online spaces.

In this book, we build on this research by exploring the ways in which ordinary working people draw resourcefully on mobile messaging apps as part of their working and social lives, thus highlighting how mobile messaging apps are deployed, alongside an array of semiotic and technological resources, as part of people's wider communicative repertoires and thus play a key part of life in the early twenty-first century.

Signposting the Book

In the next chapter, 'Post-digital Ethnography and the Networked Individual', we introduce the blend of online and offline linguistic ethnography that underlies, enables and shapes our study of mobile communication. We focus on the fact that our investigation of mobile messaging interactions is situated not within an 'online ethnography' as such but within an *offline* one – in other words, we collected digital data as part of an ethnography which was otherwise conducted offline. This approach facilitates a particular perspective on the mobile messaging data, centred round the everyday interactions and physical activities of the contemporary networked individual who sits at the intersection of overlapping social networks. Ours is a holistic approach which aims to explore the totality of the individual repertoire, as realised in the varied encounters and experiences of a person's everyday life, including those mediated by the mobile phone. In this chapter, we situate our study within the wider move from ethnography to digital ethnography to what we call post-digital ethnography, focusing particularly on the question of context, before outlining the details of our project design.

Chapter 3, 'Mobile Resourcefulness', outlines the theoretical underpinning of the book. In this chapter, we introduce our concept of *mobile resourcefulness* as a way of explaining mobile-mediated interactions. Mobile resourcefulness as we see it is not so much to do with resourcefulness in a lay sense (the ability to overcome challenges), but rather relates to the ways in which people draw on available semiotic and technological resources in response to communicative demands and real-world goals. Our aim is not to distinguish 'resourceful' from 'non-resourceful' uses but rather to explore the different ways in which resourcefulness – the ability to exploit resources in immediately relevant ways – manifests itself in otherwise mundane everyday practices. The concept of mobile resourcefulness builds on existing thinking around resourcefulness and agency, and works to explain how the *remediation* (Bolter and Grusin 2000) of social and communicative practices is driven and shaped by users' habitus, agency, purposes and normative orientations, as well as the immediate spaces – both virtual and physical – in which mediated interactions take place.

In Chapter 4, 'Polymedia Repertoires', we explore the relationship between resourcefulness and Madianou and Miller's (2012) theory of polymedia. In polymedia environments, an individual's communicative and social practices are not restricted to one social media platform, but involve the meaningful selection of affordances, combinations of different media, and movement between social media platforms. Polymedia thus requires users to draw on their language/media ideologies (Gershon 2010) – their beliefs regarding the particular communicative roles fulfilled by different platforms in the wider media environment. We show that twenty-first-century communication involves considerations of complex intersections of communicative resources at different levels of expression by drawing on our concept of the *polymedia repertoire* (Tagg and Lyons 2021), which recognises the full extent of semiotic and technological resources available to individuals in making meaning.

Chapter 5, 'Sharing in Mobile Conversations', engages in detailed analysis of our interactional data to explore how interpersonal relationships are mediated through sharing multimedia and multimodal resources such as hyperlinks, images and videos and the use of in-built platform resources such as emoji. We argue that acts of sharing and showing appreciation can be understood in terms of mobile resourcefulness because they enable networked individuals in contemporary society to uphold existing friendships and to carry out a range of social activities through exploiting the new and emerging graphic resources made available through mobile messaging. Our analysis shows how a new interactional dynamic emerges from users' practices in this context, one which acknowledges interactants' parallel engagements across online and offline spaces by suspending the typical obligation to respond and reciprocate, while also foregrounding the importance of showing attentiveness as an interactional resource.

Finally, in the conclusion (Chapter 6), we take an overall look at mobile phone users' resourcefulness across the contexts and case studies discussed in this book. In doing so, we recap the various communicative needs that prompt people to take up mobile apps, the particular contexts in which they do so, and how their practices are remediated and reshaped through the use of new mobile affordances and (networked) semiotic resources. We also explore the scope and limits of mobile resourcefulness as a way of understanding contemporary mobile practices, and flag it up as an act of everyday resistance; that is, a way in which ordinary people can resist being positioned by others – by corporations, social media companies, advertisers – and exploit technologies for their own situated and collaborative purposes.

2 Post-digital Ethnography and the Networked Individual

Introduction

During our fieldwork, we collected a series of mobile messages sent between Marta, a Polish-born actor and artist in London, and her two Polish-speaking university friends. Figure 2.1 shows part of a conversation which takes place while Marta and Marek are making their way across

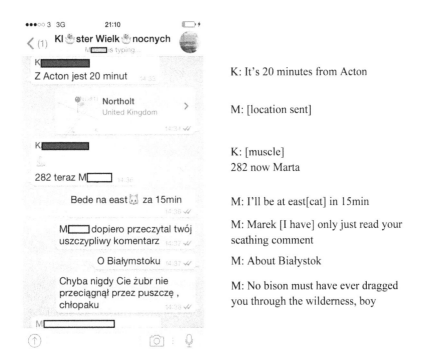

K: It's 20 minutes from Acton

M: [location sent]

K: [muscle]
282 now Marta

M: I'll be at east[cat] in 15min

M: Marek [I have] only just read your scathing comment

M: About Białystok

M: No bison must have ever dragged you through the wilderness, boy

Figure 2.1 Interweaving of the digital and the non-digital.

DOI: 10.4324/9780429031465-2

London to Klara's, who sends directions and encouragement. The extract offers a striking illustration of the way in which the digital and non-digital interweave in contemporary society.

In this digitally mediated exchange, the non-digital world is made relevant in at least two ways. Firstly, the exchange is grounded in the shifting spatial and temporal contexts of the three interlocutors as they move through the city, periodically asking for directions and updating each other on their respective locations, for example, by explicitly mentioning the distance of a named location from the target ('It's 20 minutes from Acton'), estimated time of arrival at a target underground station ('I'll be at east[cat] in 15 minutes'), contextual advice on the appropriate transport ('[bus number] 282 now Marta'), and by drawing on the affordances of the technology to share their current location on a map. Enabled by the portability of the mobile phone, the digital exchange runs parallel to the non-digital activity, both narrating their physical journeys and facilitating them. Secondly, the exchange is also intertwined with the friends' shared communicative histories and existing relationships – as evident in the way they address each other – and their wider identities as Polish people in the UK. The earlier-mentioned *east[cat]*, for example, is a multilingual and multimodal play on the name of a London underground station, Eastcote, which draws on phonetic parallels between the pronunciation of its second part – *cote* – in English and the Polish word *kot*, meaning 'cat' – an arbitrary and playful connection which indexes the interactants' shared backgrounds as language-aware Polish speakers living in London. Earlier, Marek made a scathing comment about Marta's hometown Białystok, to which she responds in an act of playful teasing, referring to the proximity of her hometown to Białowieża Forest, home to 800 European bison, Europe's heaviest land animal. The reference to Marta's origin demonstrates the friends' familiarity with each other's backgrounds, as well as Poland-focused identification and banter choices characteristic of people who share cultural knowledge. In this digitally mediated exchange, the interlocutors are thus indexing group identity and intimate relationships which extend beyond the digital space. The widely recognised implication of such data for researchers of online communication is that the digital cannot be separated from the non-digital, thus signalling the need for a blended ethnographic approach which draws on 'offline data to make sense of online phenomena' (Orgad 2009). Our departure from previous research lies in our attempt not only to use offline data such as interviews and observation to understand what we observe in digital exchanges, but to explore what the digital data can tell us about the non-digital; to respond to Bolander and Locher's (2020: 7) contention that we may also 'need online data to make sense of offline phenomena'.

In this chapter, we introduce the blend of online and offline linguistic ethnography that underlies, enables and shapes our study of mobile resourcefulness. We focus on the fact that our investigation of mobile messaging interactions is situated not within an 'online ethnography' as such but within an *offline* one – in other words, that we collected digital data as part of an ethnography which was otherwise conducted offline. This approach facilitates a particular perspective on mobile messaging data, centred round the everyday interactions and physical activities of the contemporary networked individual who sits at the intersection of overlapping social networks. Ours is a holistic approach, an extension of Silverstein's (1985) 'total linguistic fact' to understand the total multi-semiotic fact of contemporary communication. In what follows, we situate our study within the wider move from ethnography to digital ethnography to what we call post-digital ethnography, focusing particularly on the question of context, before outlining our project design.

From Ethnography to Digital Ethnography

The TLANG project contributes to a growing body of work which seeks to capture and understand social and communicative practices across offline and online spaces through ethnography. The decision to call our approach 'post-digital' recognises the limitations of carrying out 'digital ethnography', given the complex ways in which offline and online activities intertwine in people's lives and are shaped by wider cultural values (Duggan 2017). The post-digital, as used here, does not refer to a time *after* digital technology, but rather to the recognition that the digital has ceased to be a salient or disruptive element in society (Barry and Dieter 2015; Cramer 2014). Everyday life is, however, deeply and fundamentally transformed by digital technologies, calling for a focus on the role of digital technologies as part of our social lives as human beings. In this section, having charted the move towards digital ethnography in language-related research, we outline the subsequent shift in methodology and conceptualisations of context towards a post-digital approach.

The history of language-related research into the internet from the 1990s typically reflects a shift from attempts to describe the language of the internet (Crystal 2001), through researchers' concern with identifying and documenting different modal varieties (elaborated on below), and towards an interest in the *users* on and behind the screen (Androutsopoulos 2008; Bolander and Locher 2020). There has also been, from the start, a concern to situate digital communication in the wider history of communication technologies (Baron 2000). Much of the mid-wave research into different online modes associated platforms or channels of communication with particular language varieties – such as the language of email (Baron 1998) or text messaging (Tagg 2009) – and sought to pinpoint how these varieties were shaped by distinct facets of each medium and the social arrangements each facilitated (Herring 2007). This research was largely screen-based and drew on text analysis of webpages and log data rather than direct contact with users. The subsequent shift in the research agenda from use to user was in part a rejection of technological determinism in favour of the notion of affordances and user agency – and the recognition that different individuals and communities might use the same platform in different ways – as well as a wider shift in focus from texts to practices. Importantly, this new focus necessitated a shift in methodology, from text analysis to approaches that draw, in different ways, on ethnographic principles and methods.

Ethnography can be defined as an attempt to gain a holistic understanding of the lives experienced by a community or group of people, seeking not to isolate social norms, cultural values, personal relationships, or everyday and institutional practices, but to explore and document their interconnectedness and complexity in a 'thick description' (Geertz 1973). Also central to ethnographic research is the self-reflexivity of the researcher, by which the self is used as 'a resource for making sense of others' (Galani-Moutafi 2000: 294; and see Goodson and Tagg 2017 for an account of TLANG's use of researcher vignettes). The ethnographic approach is contextually contingent and thus multiple, varied and shifting, but has traditionally involved an anthropologist's long-term immersion – or 'deep hanging out' (Clifford 1997) – in a particular place (such as a village in traditional anthropological research or, more recently, a neighbourhood or institution). As Hine (2000: 46) points out, travelling to and physically 'being there' in a particular place is key to the authority of the ethnographer's interpretation. Also key to traditional conceptions of ethnography is participation (Hammersley and Atkinson 1995), which enables ethnographers to test interpretations through interaction. As we shall see later in the chapter, this focus on physical place and active participation throws up issues for ethnographies conducted online.

Ethnographies typically draw on multiple methods in constructing and investigating datasets. Research tools include observation, supported by fieldnotes, interviews, group discussions or focus groups, surveys and document analysis. The growing importance of the interview alongside observation in ethnographic research (Skinner 2012) reflects in part the ethnographic aim to achieve an emic perspective, to make central people's own understandings of their values and practices. According to Miller, D. (2016), the use of interview may also be motivated by growing difficulties in conducting participant observation in countries like the UK where people are more likely to spend time in private homes, which are typically less readily accessible to the researcher, than public community spaces (Hockey 2002). For example, as part of the global anthropological project, *Why we post*, Miller, D. (2016) notes that the England site (two villages in south-east England collectively known as 'The Glades') was perhaps 'the least ethnographic' of the studies (which included fieldsites in China, Turkey, India and Brazil, among others), given the reluctance of the English participants to hang out with a stranger and the lack of social connections between neighbours: 'developing a relationship with one household in The Glades very rarely meant any kind of interaction with anyone else' (Miller, D. 2016: 16) and as a result the researcher chose not to live in the site, like his colleagues in their respective fieldsites, and relied on going door-to-door to ask for interviews. Such experiences may require ethnographers to question their assumptions as to what constitutes a community space and refine their approach accordingly. As we discuss below, interviews have played an important role in many digital ethnographies as researchers seek to respond flexibly to the virtual research context, in particular the perceived limits of online participation, and to gain insights into log data collected online.

The various terms used to describe digital ethnography – including 'virtual ethnography' (Hine 2000), 'internet ethnography' (boyd 2008), 'netnography' (Kozinets 2009) – reflect the different ways in which ethnographic methods and/or principles have been adapted to the internet, depending on the research focus as well as the extent to which researchers conceive of ethnography as a set of methods or an epistemological approach (Varis 2016). Back in 2000, Hine (2000: 65) argued that virtual ethnography was inevitably partial and not 'quite the real thing' but rather 'an adaptive ethnography which sets out to suit itself to the conditions in which it finds itself' (cf. Georgakopoulou 2017). Since then, many digital ethnographies have started from the premise that their aim is to transfer existing methods to digitally mediated contexts, and to adapt them in ways that meet the challenges of a new research environment. For example, the core tenet of participant observation has been reworked as a form of 'systematic observation' (Androutsopoulos 2008) which involves researchers regularly visiting, surfing or lurking online. As Kytölä and Androutsopoulos (2014) show in a study of Finnish football forums, 'being there' over time can provide valuable insights into the emergence of shared practices, but unlike observation in physical settings, the researcher does not necessarily gain access to the production of online text or see interactions as they unfold in real time. Also unlike 'offline' observation, digital ethnographers can assume the role of a 'lurker', reading messages and posts but not posting their own (e.g., Lenihan's 2014 study of Facebook translators) and are thus invisible to other users; they are also relatively free to slip away from the site without disrupting it and to spend time in the field on long, reflective notes – what Mackenzie (2017) in her study of Mumsnet calls 'memos' to distinguish from more hastily scribbled fieldnotes. With the growing use of mobile devices such as smartphones, the role of the digital or mobile ethnographer is shifting again, with researchers observing how mobile-mediated exchanges intertwine with other social interactions and activities as participants move across physical spaces (Nordquist 2017). Digital ethnography, then, becomes a matter of incorporating consideration of mobile-mediated interactions into investigation of participants' physical settings. In this light, we might more profitably see the development of digital ethnography as an opportunity to revisit ethnographic assumptions. Ethnography is inherently adaptable to new conditions, shifting in response to the particular demands of any one research context and to wider shifts in epistemological approach. This includes the move from exploring remote, or 'exotic', cultures to more familiar sites of interaction and, more recently, the shift to the internet, initially as accessed through desktop computers and latterly through mobile phone apps. One perceived challenge of researching the internet is, as Page et al. (2014) put it, that 'life online is not characterised by isolated, physically distinct spaces. Rather, it is commonly thought of as highly connected and interactive' (p. 105) and 'in contrast to geographically-based field sites, may be "ambient" in nature' (p. 107). However, as boyd (2008) points out, rather than disrupting the ethnographic presumption that research takes place in a bounded, isolated setting, digital ethnography makes visible and urgent the already growing recognition of the impact of global forces and networks on local cultural dynamics, even in 'offline' ethnographies of small villages (Appadurai 1996; Piot 1999). In other words, digital ethnography highlights the fact that social life is never bounded within one physical context but is always characterised by mobility and networks that transcend particular spaces, and that encounters in physical spaces can also be ambient and fleeting. Much of the attempt to redesign ethnographies for the digital age lies in grappling with this changed concept of context, as prompted by the internet and the mobile phone.

The Question of Context in a Digital Age

Context is central to ethnography (as it is to language study) not only in the sense that ethnography involves engagement in the lives of real people in 'real-life' contexts (Papen 2005), but because ethnography is traditionally sensitive to context, in the sense that ethnographers seek to understand the context of interaction as a dynamic social category, rather than taking it for granted as existing *a priori* to any communicative action. This focus on context has, unsurprisingly, proved problematic for digital ethnographers, given the complexities of context in online environments, both conceptually (in considering what context is and what it consists of) and methodologically (in considering how a 'fieldsite' can be identified and demarcated).

Such questions have dominated digital ethnography from its emergence in the 1990s. One of the main challenges, as raised by Hine (2000), has been the extent to which digitally mediated spaces must be understood as cultures in their own right – with their own sets of norms and practices and therefore their own contexts. Alternatively, the internet and mobile phone can be understood as 'cultural artefacts'; that is, tools or resources situated within people's wider 'offline' lives and identity projects, and collectively imbued with cultural meaning. The answer may be a bit of both – digital spaces generate their own culture, but one embedded in and informed by the physical contexts in which online interactants are situated. Further, taking into account the nature of online interactions as taking place between remotely located interactants, who themselves could be engaged in a range of – offline and online – activities and spaces (Jones 2008), understanding of context in digital ethnography, with all its constituents and their interplay within and across individual interactive spaces, requires new, sophisticated approaches (Lyons 2014). Currently, however, the prioritisation of one conceptualisation or the other is often realised in the choice between a screen-based ethnography that 'treats cyberspace as the ethnographic reality' (Ducheneaut 2010: 202) or one that combines or blends screen-based and 'offline' research, typically interviews (Androutsopoulos 2008). To some extent, the choice depends on the research focus and questions, and the particular online environment being explored, but it is also possible to trace a shift in thinking over time.

Early research into online communities such as that by Baym (1993), Rheingold (1993), Reid (1991) and Danet (2001) tended to approach the internet as a new culture distinct from other elements of users' lives, albeit one that was described and evaluated in relation to 'real life'. The focus was often on identity play, as online participants discarded their 'offline' identities in the disembodied worlds of internet forums and online games and sought to take on new online personae, freed from the social constraints of their physical lives (Turkle 1995). A similar approach was taken by Boellstoroff (2008), who argued in his study of the immersive virtual world Second Life that it should not be assumed that non-digital practices or values necessarily informed digital ones, a claim based on the argument that people using Second Life did not otherwise know each other or have any contact outside the virtual environment. By immersing themselves in the online space, and not seeking to interact with the participants online, these researchers upheld the traditional ethnographic privileging of 'observation of behaviour, not simply ... the claims and accounts about people's behaviour that one would find from surveys, questionnaires and focus groups' (Miller, D. 2016: 17). From this starting point, these and other ethnographies have played a valuable role in highlighting the complexities of online life, and challenging straightforward assumptions about the effect of technology on behaviour, countering claims for either (to use Sundén's 2003 terms) 'realistic determinism' (in which the internet recreates the 'real') or 'post-modern utopianism' (in which the internet is relieved of real-world concerns) by focusing on actual cultural practices and situated experiences (boyd 2008).

Nonetheless, it appears increasingly difficult to maintain the position that life online can be understood in isolation from other contexts. As boyd (2008) points out in response to Boellstoroff's claims, many Second Life users do meet people on the platform with whom they go on to have 'offline' relationships (Au 2008) and it is not unlikely that they might meet fellow Second Lifers in other web spaces (Parks and Floyd 1996; Rheingold 1993; Taylor 2006). As ethnographers have gone on to show, digital technologies are often literally embedded in physical places (such as the webcam in the homes of Trinidadians in Miller and Sinanan's 2014 study); artefacts, people and practices move between online and offline environments (Domingo 2014; Kelty 2008; Peuronen 2011); people's online personae draw on and recontextualise their offline identities in complex ways (Kendall 2002; Jonsson and Mauranen 2014); and both offline and online practices are structured by the same wider cultural values (Miller, D. 2016; Wakeford 2003; Takahashi 2010, 2014). As an example of the latter, Takahashi (2014) shows how young Japanese people's use of social media can be understood with reference to the Japanese emic concepts of *uchi* (a sense of belonging without which an individual is nothing) and *kuuki* (the atmosphere of a situation), explaining their preference for relatively closed online spaces as the desire to create and manage an intimate *uchi*. These culture-based online preferences can be compared to the mobile messaging exchanges between Marta and her London-based Polish friends at the start of the chapter (Figure 2.1). These too require consideration of the shared histories and complex cultural identifications of the interactants for their accurate understanding.

More recent social and technological developments have tended to further break down any perceived distinction between the online and offline. Research into social media sites shows how sites such as Facebook tend to make visible and sustain existing social networks online, as users connect with people they already know (boyd and Ellison 2008; Tagg et al. 2017). At the same time, research into communication mediated by mobile phones highlights how mobile exchanges are often embedded into ongoing physical activities, revealing the extent to which people move in and out of online interactions – and between the discourses, identities and beliefs made relevant in different spaces (Lyons and Tagg 2019; and see Marta's exchange with her Polish friends as they make their way across London). Digital communication is thus seen as being entwined with offline contexts, and anchored in individuals' offline activities and ongoing identity concerns. Increasingly, studies which never set out to explore online or mobile practices have found them to be highly relevant to their participants' practices – see, for example, Singh's (2016) study of rap in Delhi and Domingo's (2014) study of rap in London. As boyd (2014: 82) said of her ethnography of online sociality among American teens, '[i]n most interviews, technology seeps in without me even having to look for it' (boyd 2014: 82).

Blending Digital Ethnographies with Non-digital Data

Hine (2000) is generally credited with pioneering a virtual ethnography approach which has shaped subsequent ethnographies taking an explicitly 'blended' approach to the construction of datasets involving digital and non-digital data. Hine used a case study – a British nanny in the United States accused of murdering a child – as a starting point for understanding the role of the internet in people's lives (in the 1990s). She took an adaptive approach to identifying and exploring a virtual fieldsite which began with webpages covering the case. These webpages were set up and maintained by private individuals and sought either to present the facts of the case or to actively support Louise. Hine then approached the website authors, sending them personalised questionnaires, following up with them in different ways – including sustained ongoing interactions in some cases – and exploring their activity across online spaces (what Androutsopoulos 2008 calls moving from the core to the periphery of the fieldsite). She also identified and investigated several Usenet newsgroups, again seeking direct contact with participants. Hine's approach has proved valuable in laying out an adaptive, multi-sited approach to identifying and exploring a cultural aspect of online behaviour, supported by direct contact with, and testimony from, the people involved.

Subsequent digital ethnographies have built on Hine's work in differing ways and in response to changing media environments. For example, boyd's (2008) ethnographic study of American teens' online sociality was similarly a multi-sited ethnography which involved long-term online, non-participant observation across online platforms, as she 'followed' young people over time from blog/journal communities such as Xanga and LiveJournal to MySpace and then to Facebook. In a departure from Hine's approach, boyd's ethnography also involved the researcher immersing herself in pop culture and travelling to states across the USA, where she hung out with teens in various public places, visited schools, and immersed herself in the local community, drawing on local census data, Google maps and visits to local landmarks. As boyd herself explains, however, it is her interviews with teens that constitute the 'bulk' of her research, 'set against online observations and observations of the communities in which these teens live' (boyd 2008: 80). She argues that 'the traces that teens leave through technology are not rich enough to convey their practices' (boyd 2014: 99) and that interviews are necessary in avoiding misinterpretations. For example, while teens' online activities might suggest a lack of regard for their own online safety, boyd's interviews with young people suggest they do care, but that networked privacy is not so much a matter of withholding information as controlling who accesses it.

More recently, ethnographers have moved away from relying only on interviews as a way of checking interpretations of the online data, not least because elicited data provides only a filter through which individuals' intentions or practices can be understood. The international anthropological project, *Why we post* (www.ucl.ac.uk/why-we-post), mentioned earlier, draws on traditional ethnographic immersion in a local context to explore the 'uses and consequences of social media', seeking to understand how social media fits into the everyday lives of people across the world. The project team identified nine research sites and adopted an ethnographic approach that suited each place. In most sites, the researcher hung out in the town or village for around 15–18 months, carrying out interviews, distributing questionnaires, working with local schools and other institutions, drawing on available public documents such as census data, and engaging in ongoing participant observation online. Among other findings, this approach enabled Miller, D. (2016) to explain local English people's use of Facebook in terms of a 'Goldilocks strategy', by which they appeared to use the site to keep people close, but not too close (in analogy with the children's fairy tale, in which Goldilocks eventually finds a bowl of porridge that is neither too hot nor too cold). The project's overall aim was to compare social media practices across the sites, with Miller explaining the Goldilocks phenomenon as a typically 'English' way of connecting with others. Such an approach recognises the ways in which individuals move between digital and non-digital spaces during their everyday lives, and that one cannot be understood in isolation from the other: in boyd's (2008: 53) own words, '[t]he offline is not simply the "backstage" to the mediated "front stage"'. These blended ethnographies situate digital communication within people's broader lives and explore how it intersects with, challenges and complements non-digital practices.

And to Digital Linguistic Ethnography

Unlike many of the ethnographies discussed above, our focus is on the use of language and other semiotic resources in online encounters.

Language-related digital ethnographic research draws on the principles established in digital ethnography to understand the appropriation and situated use of semiotic resources and discursive practices in the course of digitally mediated interactional encounters. Such work draws also on the linguistic ethnography tradition established by Rampton et al. (2004), Creese and Blackledge (2011) and Tusting and Maybin (2007), which combines ethnographic methods and principles with the tools of discourse analysis to explore how everyday acts of languaging perform identity and relational work which in turn contribute to reproducing wider social structures. In digital linguistic ethnography, the concern is with how individuals and communities exploit the perceived affordances of digitally mediated spaces – for example, the possibility of real-time interaction with distanced interactants and the availability of online global flows of commercial and cultural artefacts – to remediate existing social practices and relationships in potentially new ways. As such, digital linguistic ethnographers are ideally placed to interrogate and interpret the digital 'traces' that boyd refers to, however impoverished they may seem.

Key to digital linguistic ethnography is the need to combine interactional log data with systematic participant observation. The discourse-oriented online ethnography proposed by Androutsopoulos (2008) advocates that systematic observation move from a core discursive site – perhaps a particular bounded and socially recognised platform such as YouTube or a more restricted space such as a Facebook group – outwards through a set of interconnections towards the periphery of the fieldsite, following the online trajectories of people, practices, discourses or semiotic resources. Systematic observation – even in the absence of direct engagement with participants (as in McLaughlin 2014; Heyd 2014; Karrebæk et al. 2014) – enables sociolinguists to interpret attested discourse practices in their wider (digital) context of use, through gaining access to the participants' interactional histories (Kytölä and Androutsopoulos 2014). However, as Androutsopoulous and Staehr (2017) point out, it is now standard practice for digital linguistic ethnographers to combine systematic observation with elicited interview data (e.g., Georgalou 2017). A particularly effective example of the use of interview in digital linguistic ethnography is Lee's (2007, 2011, 2014) research, which explores how a group of bilingual undergraduate students in Hong Kong deploy their multiple linguistic resources online. Her research combines online observation and 'technobiographic' interviews which elicit life stories focused on individuals' changing relationships and experiences with technologies. The interviews include 'screen recording sessions' in which participants go online followed by questions on their current practices and daily routines, as well as their history of technology use in different phases of life (Lee 2014: 97).

In their argument for going beyond digitally mediated interactional data, Dovchin et al. (2018) make parallels between digital analysis and linguistic landscape research, which has traditionally relied on textual analysis of written signs. Alongside the 'more readily available' interactional data, Dovchin et al. (2018: 45) argue that elicited data is a necessary complement in order to gain insights into the wider context in which an online text is produced: the 'pretextual histories, contextual factors and posttextual interpretations'.

Increasingly, however, there is an acknowledgement of the need to situate digital communications within individuals' wider communicative practices and to capture the ways in which individuals move across and between online and offline spaces. Jonsson and Muhonen (2014) propose a sociolinguistic online ethnography in which digital data is combined with traditional ethnographic techniques, including observation across offline spaces. They employ this approach to explore how Swedish adolescents' Facebook activities both reflect and extend their wider affiliations, for example with Japanese culture through manga. In their study of young adults at the global periphery in Bangladesh and Mongolia, Dovchin et al. (2018) engaged not only in online observation on Facebook, but also hung out with the students during their free time, asked them to record themselves, held informal discussions with them, and interviewed them repeatedly, in order to explore how their playful transglossic practices – expressions of voice which often challenge established social and linguistic boundaries – emerged from the intersections between socio-economic background and digital participation. In a three-year, mobile, multi-sited ethnography, Nordquist (2017) followed students across their everyday movements between home, educational institutions, workplaces, social media, in transit and elsewhere, to unpack the complex ways in which these students exploited multiple literacies and resources to conform to, and challenge, dominant conventions, and how their literacy practices were informed by their wider backgrounds, beliefs and aspirations. A multi-sited mobile research design was also used to explore the interplay between the online and offline practices of an ethnically diverse group of Copenhagen adolescents who attended an urban school from 2009 to 2011 (Stæhr 2015, 2016; Madsen et al. 2016). The project included ethnographic participant observation and recordings across everyday contexts including school classes and breaktimes, leisure-time activities on the street and at youth club, and on social media, particularly Facebook, alongside semi-structured interviews and group conversations. It is within this emerging body of blended ethnographic research – focused on understanding digital interactions as part of people's wider semiotic repertoires and practices – that we situate and distinguish our 'post-digital' approach.

TLANG: Participants, Data and Methodology

The mobile messaging datasets which form the basis of this book were constructed as part of a four-year linguistic ethnography led by Angela Creese, 'Translation and Translanguaging: Investigating Linguistic and Cultural Transformations in Superdiverse Wards in Four UK Cities' (TLANG).[1] The project explored how multilingual people adapt, exploit and extend their diverse linguistic resources when working and living in superdiverse neighbourhoods, and was conducted in four UK cities: Birmingham, Cardiff, Leeds and London. The research was divided into four phases: business, heritage, sports and law. For each phase, the local city teams selected a key participant (KP) who worked in that area (e.g., business or sport).

The ethnographic approach adopted in the project involved the compilation of a range of datasets. Researchers observed KPs at work over four months and made extensive fieldnotes. They audio-recorded and interviewed participants and took photos around the site. KPs were also given audio recorders to take home and record their interactions with friends and families. Digital data formed part of this 'home data' collection stage. KPs selected and submitted examples of their social media posts and digital messages. Although we were open to receiving any form of digital material, in the main, our participants chose to share interactions mediated by their mobile phones, and particularly a range of mobile messaging apps, including SMS, WhatsApp, WeChat, Viber and Facebook Messenger, although we also received emails and accessed some participants' Facebook and other social media profiles. Most participants primarily used a mobile phone, rather than a laptop or computer, although some had access to the latter at work or home. Our methods of digital data collection varied across the project, but in most cases involved either the KP or researcher taking screenshots of KPs' phones. KPs were instructed to only submit messages they felt comfortable sharing, rather than feeling obliged to submit messages which they saw as sensitive or private (the submitted data thus reflects to some extent our participants' decisions regarding what constituted appropriate or interesting data). Data selectivity can be problematic but may be inevitable if research is to be conducted ethically and participants are empowered to make decisions (Tagg 2012; Tagg et al. 2017). In the case of the TLANG project, digital data collection was a new element added to an established methodological approach, and so the methods were exploratory and responsive, particularly as data collection relied on the nature of the relationships established between the team and each participant. The establishment of relationships of trust between researcher and researched was key to finding a way into the digital data and was therefore central to the authority we could then claim for our interpretations (Hine 2000).

Post-digital and the Networked Individual

The TLANG project design allows for a particular *blended linguistic ethnography* approach which recognises the conditions of post-digital society; that is, one in which digital technologies have ceased to be a novel or disruptive influence but are instead experienced as an inherent part of being human (Cramer 2014) – extending or transforming what we think of as human in ways that incorporate the digital (McLuhan 1964). In a post-digital society, digital technologies are embedded in wider social practices and relationships and intertwined with offline activities and physical contexts (Marsh 2019), while semiotic repertoires are structured and organised around the intersections between language and media choices (Lexander and Androutsopoulos 2021; Tagg and Lyons 2021). Our post-digital ethnographic approach not only assumes the importance of understanding online interactions within the context of the physical settings in which they take place but also recognises the role that digital interactions have in shaping people's offline activities, personal relationships and language ideologies.

The approach builds on existing digital linguistic ethnographies discussed above, which combine online data with interviews and (sometimes) offline observations to gain an emic understanding of people's online lives (Androutsopoulos 2008; Georgalou 2017). There are clear parallels between our blended approach and research which combines online and offline observations (Dovchin et al. 2018; Miller, D. 2016; Nordquist 2017). Our methodology departs from this research in terms of the balance between, and prioritisation afforded, the offline and online data. Rather than combining offline and online ethnography or using non-digital data to inform digital ethnography, we collected digital data as part of an otherwise offline ethnography; that is, we did not observe people online or immerse ourselves in the online context but in our participants' physical settings at work and at home. In other words, digital data was collected as part of an ethnography which took place offline (through offline observations and fieldnotes) with consideration of what participants were doing in parallel online channels. Importantly, our project design prompted us to interpret the digital data not primarily in the context of its online setting but rather in the context of the individual's wider milieu, offline activities and social networks. Unlike other studies of social media and language use – such as Androutsopoulos's (2008) discourse-centred online ethnography – we used ethnography neither to understand life as it occurs online nor to inform people's online practices through insights gathered in offline contexts, but rather to explore individuals' (networked) practices across the many social spaces they inhabit, including online ones; that is, to understand digital practices as part of individuals' lived experiences across contexts and as part of their wider communication practices. Our research explored how people's uptake of digital technologies is both shaped by, and goes on to shape, their social lives as human beings.

The project design also enabled us to develop an approach to identifying and demarcating a fieldsite which crosses multiple offline contexts and online platforms by orienting our research around the *networked individual* – an individual who sits as a node at the centre of a complex of overlapping social and material networks (Papacharissi 2011). While other ethnographies have taken *space* as their starting point – focusing, for example, on a workspace such as a market or kitchen (Pennycook and Otsuji 2015) or a platform such as Facebook (Georgalou 2017) – our focus on the networked individual usefully highlights the ways in which digital interactions cut across spheres of life and blur the boundaries between them, as well as the ways in which individuals move between different digital platforms (Adami 2014). This focus enables us to shift from a primary concern with the affordances and constraints of any one platform or online space towards an understanding of the different ways in which networked individuals exploit affordances across multiple non-digital and digital spaces in achieving communicative purposes. In focusing on the individual and moving out through their networks and encounters, we draw not only on Lee's (2014) 'techno-biographic' approach in using interviews to make sense of an individual's online practices, but also on offline observations and fieldnotes to provide a holistic understanding of individuals' communicative practices and how they vary across online and offline contexts.

For individuals, being 'networked' transforms the potential for performing the self and making connections across traditionally distinct social spheres (Papacharissi 2011). Firstly, networked individuals are connected to distributed others within complex online social networks. Social networks (Milroy 1987) – patterns of relationships grounded in local contexts – are extended through digital technologies across sometimes vast geographical distances in virtual space (Heyd 2014). The configuration of an online social network, and how it intersects with offline connections, has implications for which semiotic and technological resources are taken up, how resources are shared and adapted across contexts, and for the development of shared media ideological understandings. Secondly, as this suggests, the socially networked individual also has access to the range of semiotic resources or artefacts (where the latter term indicates more complex pre-assembled semiotic constructions) which circulate both locally and globally through an individual's digital connections: 'an endless flow of digital linguistic material, which networked actors can explore, appropriate and recontextualise' (Androutsopoulos 2015: 189). Such digital resources can be likened to objects in a material space, which become communicatively meaningful as participants engage with them (Kusters et al. 2017: 226).

Pennycook (2018: 452) argues that, like material artefacts, distributed virtual artefacts are themselves interactants in online interactional encounters, shaping not only our access to semiotic resources but also, by extension, how we relate to others, and what we can do and think. For example, the flow of information and how this is managed within and across online social networks is pivotal in shaping processes of (dis)identification (Leppänen et al. 2014) – how people position themselves and others – as well as redefining notions of individual privacy as 'increasingly networked' (boyd 2012: 348). Reconceptualising the individual as networked thus highlights how an individual's digital interactions are always reliant on the ways in which available resources are taken up within the webs of people's complex social connections.

Analysing the Data

Data analysis was a team endeavour with multiple iterative stages, each of which took place for each city case study and was repeated for each thematic phase (business, heritage, sport, law). The first stage comprised a broad reading of the datasets collected around one networked individual, including audio recordings and transcriptions across home and work contexts, fieldnotes, interviews, linguistic landscape photos and digital, largely mobile-mediated, interactions. Themes running across these datasets were identified and elaborated on in a series of project reports, themselves summarised in working papers housed on our website (those particularly useful in the writing of this book are Blackledge et al. 2015, 2016, 2017, 2018; Zhu Hua et al. 2015, 2016). These reports were shared and the findings discussed at regular team events, with broader themes emerging across datasets. For example, one recurrent theme that emerged was the role of the body in face-to-face encounters (Blackledge and Creese 2018; Callaghan et al. 2018; Zhu Hua et al. 2017). Our endeavour to work as a team and to benefit from the diversity of perspectives, experiences and expertise that team members brought with them created a multivoiced layered process of knowledge co-construction (discussed further in Goodson and Tagg 2017).

The second stage involved a foregrounding of the digital data, informed by the preceding and wider analyses and by our ethnographic experience in the fieldsites (see working papers Tagg 2015; Tagg et al. 2016, 2018; Tagg and Hu 2017). We were aware throughout the process of the need to balance our holistic 'post-digital' approach – which placed digital interactions on a par with any other interactions in which individuals engaged – with the need to extract and isolate the digital data to identify and explore the contribution of digitally mediated encounters to these individuals' semiotic repertoires and communicative practices. Rather than transcribing the digital data, we worked with the original screenshots – albeit in anonymised form and with parallel translations into English where necessary – to maintain as much as possible the original context of the interactions. We analysed the digital data in various ways and from multiple perspectives, guided by the overall project themes and research questions, as well as the literature and the emergent salient themes mentioned above. Our digital discourse analyses drew on the principles of interactional sociolinguistics, which explores how meaning is co-constructed in social interaction (Gumperz 1999; Gumperz and Hymes 1972). Interactional sociolinguistics – a field which encompasses a range of methods and theoretical ideas – involves micro-analysis of unfolding interactions and seeks to understand how wider social structures, cultural phenomena and linguistic patterns emerge from, and are reproduced in, these everyday interactional practices. Although interactional sociolinguistics is traditionally concerned with naturally occurring spoken interaction, studies have shown that digitally mediated exchanges can be fruitfully analysed by drawing on and adapting the tools developed for face-to-face real-time interactions (Herring 2004, 2018). Our analysis of our participants' mobile communication sheds light on the ways in which people draw on, align and negotiate their communicative repertoires to make social meaning within interactional encounters mediated by mobile phone messaging, and the implications such encounters have for their wider relationships, identity projects and social and professional activities. In this book, we draw on selected data extracts to illustrate aspects of the emergent theme of mobile resourcefulness: polymedia, multimodality, sharing.

The Ethical Implications of a Post-digital Ethnography

For the ethical researcher, ethnography goes beyond what has been described as 'macro-ethics' – compliance with institutional ethical procedures – and aims to address local dilemmas and decisions as they arise throughout a research project in a responsive and contextually sensitive process – a form of 'micro-ethics' or 'ethics of care' (Kubanyiova 2008; cf. Markham and Buchanen 2015). The research aim of the TLANG project – to develop a holistic understanding of the totality of semiotic repertoires across the varied encounters and experiences of a person's everyday life – is driven by the moral imperative to recognise and celebrate the resourceful, multilingual human, to provide a platform for those individuals whose voices are not often heard in public debate, and to contribute in positive ways to policy and practice through partnership with non-academic organisations. The project design, and the particular blend of digital and non-digital, nonetheless led us to a series of critical ethical junctures that are explored in greater length in Tagg et al. (2017) and which were discussed extensively, along-side other ethically important moments, at team meetings throughout the project (see also Markham and Buchanen 2015; Spilioti and Tagg 2017, 2022). These critical moments arose in part from the ways in which mobile technologies expanded the boundaries of the 'offline' research field (albeit one that already encompassed multiple interconnected sites), involving in our research geographically far-flung interactants with whom the research team had no direct contact, and making relevant online contexts in which we were not immersed. This had practical implications for how we gained consent from these interactants (usually through our key participants) and for their understanding of the potential implications of participation.

In contrast to this distancing effect, our use of mobile technologies in organising observations and meetings with our participants often had the effect of enhancing intimacy between researcher and researched, blurring the lines between professional and personal relationships, and between what might be considered data and what was personal communica-tion (Bhattacharya 2007). This had potential implications both for us as researchers and for our participants after we had withdrawn from the field and from their lives. Our ethical handling of the digital data was further complicated by the contrasting ways in which participants and researchers viewed the former's mediated interactions. To many of our participants, their digitally mediated interactions were mundane, trivial and ephemeral, despite the team's perception of some interactions as sensitive or private (and our awareness of the potential permanence of published data), and this meant that, on occasion, the team decided to override participants' agency in granting us access to data which we decided not to use or publish (Tagg et al. 2017). Such decisions, while driven by our commitment to an ethics of care, inevitably shape the stories we tell about the encounters and practices of the networked individuals in our study.

Conclusion

This chapter outlined the methodological approach which guides the find-ings reported and discussed in subsequent chapters in this book. Our blend of digital and non-digital data – what we call 'post-digital' in its attempt to incorporate the digital as an inherent part of being human in contemporary society – had an important bearing on our decision to focus on resourceful-ness in relation to our participants' use of their mobile phones, by prompting us to look to the role that digitally mediated communication played in our participants' wider networked lives. Although, as this chapter has shown, our approach aligns with and builds on a wider trend within digital ethnog-raphies to challenge traditionally conceived boundaries between the online and offline, our project design nonetheless simultaneously restricts us from exploring other angles of possible research – we do not, for example, interview all participants in the digitally mediated interactions nor participate in their unfolding over time – in other words, our tendency is to focus on a mobile messaging interaction as a cultural artefact situated in a particular place and time rather than as an emerging culture of its own (Hine 2000). What our approach enables and constrains in terms of analysis should be borne in mind throughout this book and in evaluating our conclusions.

Note

1 AHRC *Translation and Translanguaging: Investigating Linguistic and Cultural Transformations in Superdiverse Wards in Four UK Cities.* (AH/L007096/1). Angela Creese (PI). With CIs Mike Baynham, Adrian Blackledge, Frances Rock, Lisa Goodson, Li Wei, James Simpson, Caroline Tagg, Zhu Hua.

3 Mobile Resourcefulness

Introduction

As a butcher in the indoor market in Birmingham, UK, Kang Chen – originally from Fujian Province in China – makes regular meat deliveries to local Cantonese restaurants. Shortly before we observed his working practices in late 2014, Kang Chen began to receive the restaurants' orders not through voice calls or on-site visits but through the mobile messaging app, WeChat, as illustrated in Figure 3.1.

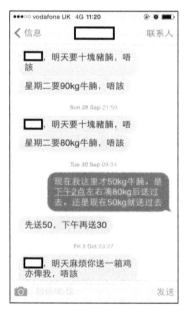

[name of stall], tomorrow send us 10 pieces of pork belly. Many thanks

Tuesday we want 90 kg beef belly, many thanks

[name of stall], tomorrow send us 10 pieces of pork belly. Many thanks

Tuesday we want 80 kg beef belly, many thanks

I only have 50kg beef belly here at the moment. Do you want us to send you 80kg at 2 o'clock this afternoon after the new delivery or 50kg to be delivered now?

Send us the 50 first, then the rest 30 in the afternoon

[name of stall], tomorrow send us a box of chicken wings, sorry for the bother. Thanks

Figure 3.1 Ordering meat on WeChat

DOI: 10.4324/9780429031465-3

This business practice is facilitated by various affordances of mobile messaging, including the portability of the mobile phone, the ability to cut and paste the same text into new messages and the convenience of asynchronicity – the restaurants use the app to leave Kang Chen messages which he can pick up in his own time (similarly, he leaves orders with his suppliers before 9 pm every evening for a delivery the following day), co-constructing what can be described as a *virtual noticeboard*. The act of writing, rather than speaking, enables them to draw on their respective habitus (Bourdieu 1977) in their use of two different but mutually intelligible scripts: Kang Chen uses the simplified script he learnt in mainland China, while the restaurant owner uses the traditional 'complicated' script taught in Hong Kong. This is an act of convenience (given their phones' respective default settings) and also one of (dis)alignment between individuals drawing on distinct yet mutually familiar political, social and cultural backgrounds, migration trajectories and social networks. Researching Kang Chen's use of the virtual noticeboard as an emergent business practice, we were struck by the extent to which it was embedded in his existing practices and contexts and, in particular, by the *resourceful* ways in which Kang Chen and his business partners took up and exploited mobile technologies to better achieve their existing goals.

In this chapter, we outline our concept of *mobile resourcefulness* as a way of understanding mobile-mediated interactions such as these. It should be clarified at the outset that *mobile* here refers to the smartphone device used by migrant entrepreneurs such as Kang Chen, rather than the *portability* of the device (see Chapter 1) or the mobility of practices and resources (Blommaert 2010), although these are central affordances of the technology and of relevance to this book. Mobile resourcefulness relates to the way in which people draw on available semiotic and technological resources in response to communicative demands and real-world goals, and how this manifests in otherwise mundane everyday practices. The concept builds on existing thinking around resourcefulness (e.g., Mavers 2007) and around agency (Ahearn 2010; Miller, E.R. 2016), and explains how the *remediation* of social and communicative practices (Bolter and Grusin 2000; Madianou and Miller 2012) is driven and shaped by users' habitus, agency, purposes and normative orientations, as well as the physical and virtual spaces in which mediated interactions take place.

After showing how remediation, resourcefulness and agency come together to shape mobile communication practices, at the end of the chapter we draw on three case studies: Kang Chen's use of WeChat to organise meat deliveries and carry out other aspects of his business, as described above; Joanne's harnessing of her social networks to conduct an informal import business through WeChat; and Winnie's realisation of personal values through WhatsApp and SMS. In each, we see how networked individuals draw on a range of communicative genres, existing semiotic resources and social networks, as well as new technological affordances, to get things done.

Remediation and Reframing

Remediation describes the uptake of new technologies not as representing radical breaks from, or transformations of, older technologies but in terms of how they remediate existing technologies (Bolter and Grusin 2000). This is often reflected in the terms used for new technologies – *webpage* for example, draws on an analogy between the web and the book (see Collins and Thompson 2020 for discussion of *scroll*). New technologies are likely to be framed or understood by designers, the broadcast media and users alike (Pennington and Birthisel 2016; Laitinen and Valo 2018) in ways that reflect perceptions and experiences of older technologies. These frames – internalised constructions through which we make sense of the world and which guide our future actions (Goffman 1974: 21) – are ideologically and socially constructed, allowing powerful individuals and institutions such as the media to impose particular interpretative frameworks and further consolidate their power (Tucker 1998). The main frames through which we view contemporary technologies often have a long history, as our experiences and existing anxieties with older technologies are remediated in encounters with newer technologies (Gitelman 2006). Dominant discourses surrounding new media – such as worries about the impact on established social order (Marvin 1988) – thus find their antecedents in the way the landline, television and video games (and so on) were once framed. Technological change from this perspective is not revolutionary but evolutionary, often incremental and deeply embedded in particular historical and cultural contexts.

Picking up on this perspective, social researchers have used remediation to explain social and communicative practices associated with new technologies. This can involve what Jones and Hafner (2012) call the 'technologisation of practice', by which technologically mediated practices come to be so strongly associated with a particular technology that social conventions grow around its use – and the technology itself becomes transparent or 'normalised' (Bax 2011). These normalised technology uses then shape how practices are carried out using new technologies. In applying remediation to their understanding of how Trinidadians use communication technologies, for example, Madianou and Miller (2012: 177) show how people initially treated webcam interactions as phone calls with video and saw email as 'computer-based letters', an observation that resonates with research in the late twentieth century which sought to determine if computer-mediated communication resembled speech or writing, or something in between (Baron 2000). Uses of new technologies are also shaped by the wider political and economic agendas of commercial companies (Tagg et al. 2017) – as well as the broadcast media – who can choose to frame a technology in ways that suit their own purposes. WeChat, for example, first became popular as a voice messaging service but is now seen by its users as the place to go to for a range of online services (Deng and Chen 2018), perhaps in part because of its subsidisation and promotion by the Chinese government who bans or censors other apps (Liao 2018).

Frames are dynamic, shifting and overlapping (Crider and Ganesh 2004), shaped by the ways in which they are interpreted and represented in interaction (Dewulf et al. 2009) and can be challenged or resisted in everyday practice, with situations eventually reframed or a new frame 'keyed' (Goffman 1974). In their Trinidadian study, Madianou and Miller (2012) show how the practices remediated through webcam and email are gradually transformed as users begin to recognise and exploit the affordances of new technologies; starting, for example, to use email for shorter, more spontaneous and less carefully crafted messages; and to use webcam to provide a window into their everyday lives. Their study illustrates how communicative practices can shift over time in response to user perceptions of the available affordances. In the case of Kang Chen, we see how an established business practice he once carried out through voice calls is remediated through WeChat, serving the same transactional purposes while subtly reconfiguring the practice by removing the need for synchronous interaction and creating a potentially more permanent record of meat orders which can be accessed at the butcher's convenience.

Over time, these changing communicative practices can lead to a shift in how new technologies are themselves framed or understood. Examples abound regarding the ways in which online platforms are reframed through the often unforeseen ways in which users take up their affordances (Hendus 2015; Levin 2017). Perceptions of the social network site Facebook, for example, were reframed (apparently against the company's will) following its alleged role in spreading fake news and manipulating political outcomes, when it was repositioned as either a media-sharing site or a publisher – with the UK Select Committee into fake news eventually proposing 'a new category of social media company, which tightens tech companies' liabilities, and which is not necessarily either a "platform" or a "publisher"' (DCMS 2018: 10). Kang Chen's use of WeChat in organising meat deliveries involved a personal reframing of an app which (at the time) he otherwise used for social purposes such as contacting his brother in China. The ways in which technologies are framed varies not only across time but across countries, organisations, social networks and individuals, depending in part on contextual and relational factors such as communicative purpose and interactants' social relationships (Laitinen and Valo 2018).

In exploring mobile phone remediation through the concept of *mobile resourcefulness*, we focus attention on the technology *users* – their communicative purposes, self-positioning and social relationships – and how and why they remediate existing practices through new technologies in ways that can reaffirm or reinterpret how a technology is framed. To do so, we draw on the literature into the *semiotic repertoire* and notions of resourcefulness in business, technology use and communication.

Resources and Resourcefulness

The idea that people draw on communicative or semiotic resources in making meaning has proven central to recent conceptualisations of communication which challenge the notion of 'languages' as either fixed or discrete entities, and which instead show how people draw more flexibly from semiotic repertoires comprising not only various languages, dialects, genres and registers, but also 'gesture, posture, how people walk, stand, and sit, the way they tilt their head, their gaze, the shrug of their shoulders, their smile or frown' (Blackledge and Creese 2018: 2) as well as such things as 'knowledge of communicative routines, familiarity with types of food or drink ... and mass media references' (Rymes 2014: 303). The term *verbal repertoire* was first used to describe the 'totality' of language varieties and registers available to a speech community (Gumperz 1964), but this focus on community norms has since shifted towards individual repertoires comprising resources that are picked up by individuals on their trajectories though life and shaped by their dynamic involvement with multiple communities or networks. As Busch (2014: 14) points out, individual repertoires exist only as 'constraints and potentialities', and are realised within the space of an interactional encounter as 'situated usages of resources, that is, practices' (Kusters et al. 2017: 222). The ways in which semiotic resources are taken up are not only shaped by the interactional dynamics between individuals (Blackledge and Creese 2018) but also emerge from the wider material and social environment: repertoires are thus 'an emergent property deriving from the interactions between people, artefacts and space' (Pennycook 2018: 454). In the context of the busy commercial spaces explored in Pennycook and Otsuji (2015), for example, these 'spatial repertoires' are shaped by noise and bustle, flows of customers, the nature of various artefacts in use and the products being sold. In mobile communication, repertoires can be shaped both by the affordances and social expectations associated with a discursively co-constructed online space and by the social norms and everyday activities of the (shifting and potentially multiple) physical contexts of each interlocutor (Lyons and Tagg 2019). In line with the above, we assume that repertoires, while shaped in part by the individual trajectories of those involved, are ultimately not the property of an individual mind but are distributed across the historical bodies, material objects, social relationships and discourses that constitute a social space. In other words, while an individual person brings to an interaction certain communicative resources (and may lack others), the resources deployed in any one communicative encounter are always the result of a process of co-construction with other people and shaped by the expectations and materiality of the communicative space. This raises questions regarding the process by which distributed resources come to be taken up and deployed in interaction, questions that our concept of resourcefulness serves, in part, to address.

In line with the conceptualisation of the distributed semiotic repertoire, our observations regarding mobile resourcefulness do not assume that people *have* resources but focus rather on how people draw on available resources – or co-construct them – to make meaning and get things done. The *Oxford English Dictionary* gives two definitions of *resourceful*, both attested since the early nineteenth century: (1) skilled in devising expedients or in meeting difficulties; full of practical ingenuity; and (2) rich in reserves or resources (OED online 2021). The latter tends to describe such things as land (rather than people), and the former is closest to our understanding of mobile resourcefulness. Resourcefulness as used across the research literature similarly refers not to novel practices or solutions but to people's ability to evaluate, select and combine existing resources appropriately to achieve contextually relevant goals, including the resolution of everyday challenges and problems (Kuijer et al. 2017), identity negotiation (Ting-Toomey 1993) and meaning-making (Mavers 2007). Importantly, if unsurprisingly, despite differences in how resourcefulness is conceptualised, the various understandings highlight human agency, initiative and intentionality – and it is in relation to this aspect that our understanding of mobile resourcefulness departs from other conceptualisations of resourcefulness.

Of relevance is research into *entrepreneurial resourcefulness*, which explores how people overcome hurdles such as a limited availability of resources in realising a vision and achieving commercial success. Corbett and Katz (2003: xi) observe that newer and smaller businesses may be able to 'target opportunities in unique ways by addressing resource gaps through novel means not available to more mature and resource munificent competitors' – in other words, business advantage may be gained through how available resources are harnessed and deployed (Mosakowski 2002; Powel and Baker 2011). While entrepreneurs can be driven to become resourceful through necessity (Welter and Xheneti 2013), the literature also assumes that some people are 'resourceful by nature' (Corbett and Katz 2003: ix–x) – that resourcefulness resides within (some) individuals. In our interviews, for example, we heard how Kang Chen and Meiyan Chew learnt to be butchers in the UK on the job and, during fieldwork, we observed them at work and at home seeking to identify or create opportunities for further growing their business (Blackledge et al. 2015). Their stories of becoming involve the endurance of physical challenges and the devising of survival strategies and, in this sense, it might be argued that the couple – as well as many of our other participants – are particularly resourceful entrepreneurs, likely driven both by nature and necessity. With a similar focus on how resources are deployed, the concept of *digital resourcefulness* emerged from recognition that access to technology is not sufficient to overcome the 'digital divide' without also taking technology *use* into account (Narjes 2018). In their household survey, Gallardo and Wiltse (2018) measured digital resourcefulness by such factors as whether respondents claimed to require help with new devices and were able to avoid online echo chambers. While the largest gap between urban and rural populations lay in their differential access to the internet, the researchers found that digital resourcefulness and utilisation were essential to enriching the internet experience (Gallardo and Wiltse 2018: 34), and they conclude that improving individuals' digital literacies is key to ensuring families benefit from digital access, again locating resourcefulness in (learnt) individual capacity for action.

Within intercultural communication studies, the notion of *communicative resourcefulness* is a key part of identity negotiation theory (Ting-Toomey 1993) for studying immigrants' or minority group members' acculturation process and identity change in unfamiliar cultural environments (Collie et al. 2010). According to this view, effective identity negotiation – in which people position themselves and others in order to ensure interaction proceeds smoothly and to achieve communicative goals and mutual understanding – requires communicative competence (Hymes 1978; Canale and Swain 1980), particularly in intercultural encounters. A 'competent' communicator is one with a great deal of communicative resourcefulness, including knowledge, motivation, skills and an ability to seek out common values (Sharapan 2016), and who draws on these resources to act 'appropriately, effectively, and creatively in any novel situation' (Ting-Tommey 1993: 90). The focus here is not so much on individuals being able to exploit resources at a textual or material level (including linguistic and other modal resources, media, tools and technologies), but rather on their acquired cognitive, behavioural and affective resources. One limitation of this is that individuals are depicted as '*a priori* agentive entities' who come to an interaction ready equipped to 'engage with … an external other' (Miller, E.R. 2016: 350). Similarly, interlocutors are seen as reaching pre-defined and anticipated communicative goals with, as Abrams et al. (2012: 228) point out, the assumption that people are primarily concerned with achieving smooth interactions rather than asserting their distinct identities. Such an assertion of identity is evident in Pinnow's (2011) case study of a Latino student in a middle school in the south-eastern United States who draws 'skillfully' (p. 390) on multiple semiotic resources – including various modal resources and his social and political knowledge – to assert himself and his cultural identity in an interactional conflict with his teacher. Our observations regarding mobile resourcefulness paint a more nuanced unfolding picture in which interlocutors negotiate multiple shared concerns – identity claims, business imperatives, relationship management – and orient towards coexisting and often competing polycentric sources of authority (Blommaert 2010) including their home culture and family, immediate business conventions and regulations, formal literacy expectations and emerging digital cultures: the brief extract from the virtual noticeboard (Figure 3.1), for example, accommodates competing orientations towards the national literacy standard of each interactant's respective origin. The resourcefulness evident in such encounters can be explained in part by the need for the migrant entrepreneurs and their interlocutors to navigate multiple identities, discourses and norms, and the role played by relatively new technologies in their doing so.

The notion of *semiotic resourcefulness*, although it has not been widely taken up in the literature, is of greatest relevance in understanding mobile resourcefulness due to its focus on using textual and material resources for meaning-making within communicative encounters. The concept, introduced by Mavers (2007), is grounded in social semiotic theory which presupposes that all acts of meaning-making are agentive because they involve choice and design processes (Kress 2010; Bezemer and Kress 2017). Mavers (2007) explicitly foregrounds agency, individual choice and contextual awareness in her discussion of semiotic resourcefulness, which she defines as 'making the most of the resources that are available for making meaning according to the immediate representational/communicational purpose' (Mavers 2007: 171).

Of particular relevance to this book is the argument that social media platforms or apps are themselves semiotic resources in the sense that the selection of medium can be socially meaningful: Mavers (2007: 162) notes that choice of, say, email over other platforms can enable certain writing-related modes and determines the pace and nature of their interaction. Madianou and Miller's (2012) theory of *polymedia* – which we return to in Chapter 4 – is useful in theorising platforms as semiotic resources. Polymedia conceptualises social media as an integrated communicative environment of platforms which each find a niche in people's communicative repertoires depending on their affordances (Madianou 2015: 2). Reinforced through use, platforms thus accrue their own social meanings and significance in relation to other platforms, which in turn shapes how networked individuals go on to use them. For example, Miller, D. (2016) finds that English teenagers increasingly perceive Facebook as a space monitored and controlled by their parents, and so migrate to Twitter which they comprehend as facilitating intimate interactions free from their parents' gaze (see also Quan-Haase and Young 2010). As explored further in Chapter 4, we argue that users' mobile resourcefulness underlies people's ability to determine the suitability of a media platform to accommodate their specific communicative needs within a framework of shared social conventions, and explains how their selection and use of this semiotic resource may change over time.

Reconceptualising Agency in Resourcefulness

As evident in the above discussion, the notion of *agency* – understood broadly as the human capacity to act (Giddens 1979) – is central to existing conceptualisations of resourcefulness. Indeed, the very point of identifying mobile resourcefulness in our participants' use of technology is to highlight their ability to make the most of their mobile phones. However, we situate mobile resourcefulness in the conceptualisation of agency articulated by Miller, E.R. (2016) as 'always relational, always distributed' (p. 354). To some extent, this reflects a more general understanding of agency across the social sciences, which does not imply the freedom to act at will but instead serves to locate the human capacity to act within larger social and political processes (Ahearn 2010: 29) and to show how social structures which constrain human action and life opportunities are themselves reproduced, challenged or potentially transformed through discourse (Swann et al. 2004).

A key constraint on agency is *habitus* – the 'internalised style of knowing and relating to the world that is grounded in the body itself' (Bourdieu 1977); a 'set of dispositions or habits that are learned throughout childhood and beyond' (Swann et al. 2004: 131) and inscribed onto the body: hence Scollon and Scollon's (2004) use of the parallel term, *historical body*. Habitus is important to understanding agency because it 'emphasises the way in which agency is mediated and shaped by the social contexts we inhabit – and which, in turn inhabit us' (Lillis 2013: 129–130). That is, how an individual is able to act in any given context is bound up in complex ways with their embodied cultural histories. In relation to technology use, an individual's bodily experience of older technologies and certain forms of social interaction may shape the frame through which they perceive and use a new technology. In their study of distance education at the University of Alaska in the 1980s, for example, Scollon and Scollon (2004: 61–62) observe how students drew on internalised understandings of familiar technology-mediated practices associated with playing computer games, rather than their past experiences of schooling, creating a playful, informal discourse in the new educational space. Although habitus tends to lead to the reproduction or reconfiguration of existing social structures, of relevance to our focus on the use of new technologies by transnational migrants is the possibility of social transformation when people act on their habitus in new social situations (Ahearn 2010: 33).

Focusing on the constraints exerted by habitus and other social and political structures on individual choices and intentions, however, obscures the more profound insight that 'taking such actions is possible only because of our social histories and is enabled only in relation to the complex ecology of affordances and constraints … that are part of our everyday circumstances' (Miller, E.R. 2016: 355). Miller holds that *agency* as 'the production of effect or action' should be distinguished from the assumption of the *agent* as 'the presumed origin of effect or action' (Lundberg and Gunn 2005: 88; cited in Miller, E.R. 2016: 352–353). Drawing on Scollon (2001), she argues that actions – often construed as emerging from an individual agent – are in fact distributed across the people, artefacts, technologies, discourses and contexts which contribute to an action (cf. Ahearn 2010: 29). In her analysis of interviews with an Indonesian man regarding his early life and migration to the USA, Miller, E.R. (2016) shows how his choices and reflexive capacities were mediated by the surrounding ideologies, discourses, affordances and interactional needs of his immediate milieu, as well as wider political, economic and social forces at multiple timescales. He was 'enabled to act at the nexus of these socially and historically constructed opportunities and obligations' (Miller, E.R. 2016: 359) – and, in so doing, reproduced existing social structures. This understanding of agency helps us to see that resourcefulness is not an individual capacity but a dispersed practice: 'constellations of interconnected elements' which not only involve people, artefacts and technologies (Kuijer et al. 2017: 190) but also the multiple material and ideological spaces in which communication is embedded (Pennycook 2018).

Considering dispersed agency in relation to the butcher Kang Chen, we see, for example, how his decision to move to the UK was embedded in local expectations, social norms and beliefs: in interview, Kang Chen attributed his eagerness to travel to 'the inspiration you gained from your village folks'; that is, the stories told by villagers who had travelled (Blackledge et al. 2015: 14). These stories were shaped themselves by economic imperatives: the Fujian province owes its prosperity in part to the remittances sent back from emigrants, which provide funds for schools and community centres, business ventures and construction projects (Keefe 2009). Meanwhile,

Kang Chen's decision to carry out meat ordering through WeChat emerged in collaboration between the butcher and the Birmingham-based restaurant owners, and was shaped by the affordances (and constraints) of the mobile phone. As pointed out at the start of the chapter, the act of digital writing encourages the interactants to engage in asynchronous communication, and enables them to replicate messages through cutting and pasting and to draw on their respective preferred script (simplified or traditional). At the same time, the default settings constrain their ability to move between scripts (or engage in trans-scripting). Drawing on our wider ethnographic data, we can argue that the virtual noticeboarding was initially enabled by Meiyan's encouragement to her husband to download WeChat in the first place, and shaped by such things as the pace of their busy working lives and the nature of the noisy spaces in which they work. Looking wider still, we can point to the economic and social necessities that drive their entrepreneurship, and the wider political and cultural forces shaping their linguistic and cultural identities and prompting their script choices.

In sum, resourcefulness implies agency – indeed, the term is used here (and elsewhere) precisely to focus on the role of human endeavour and action within a sociocultural space – however, agency should not be understood as the human capacity to act independently and intentionally, but rather as distributed and emergent. This understanding of agency enables us to recognise resourcefulness as a human trait but not one that necessarily originates solely in the human. Understood in this way, the concept of resourcefulness can shed light on the processes by which spatial semiotic repertoires come to be harnessed and deployed by interlocutors in the course of unfolding interactions, in the collaborative pursuit of communicative goals shaped by habitus and life histories, material constraints and ideological positionings.

Mobile Resourcefulness and Remediation

This understanding of resourcefulness allows us to return to the concept of remediation to explore how and why social and communicative practices are remediated through new technologies and how and why these technologically mediated practices might change. In short, the concept of mobile resourcefulness puts the *user* at the centre of processes of remediation, drawing attention to the way in which technological change is driven and shaped by its users, albeit those whose agency emerges from the wider sociocultural contexts in which they are situated. Drawing on Ahearn's (2010) definition of agency and Mavers' (2007) conceptualisation of semiotic resourcefulness, we propose an understanding of *mobile resourcefulness* as the *socioculturally situated capacity to make the most of distributed semiotic resources associated with the mobile phone in accordance with contextual circumstances and towards some communicative or social end.* As in Giddens' definition, this understanding of agency does not imply that individuals necessarily have consciously articulated goals in mind (Giddens 1979) but rather invokes, in Duranti's (2006: 36) words, the '"aboutness" of our mental and physical activity'. This definition enables us to explore how the remediation of social and communicative practices is shaped by the varied ways in which people – as socioculturally situated, networked individuals – draw on, curate and negotiate linguistic, multimodal and multimedia resources in dealing with new technologies and, in the case of most of our participants, in relatively unfamiliar and rapidly changing social situations in their host country.

The role of mobile resourcefulness in the remediation of communicative practices involves a non-linear and iterative process which moves between the following elements or stages.

- The theory starts from the assumption that technologically mediated social change is always embedded in existing contexts and practices, as people experience and respond to varied and fluctuating communicative and social needs and purposes.
- New or adapted technologies (such as the mobile phone and/or a mobile phone app and/or a functionality within that app) are collaboratively adopted by people when their affordances are perceived to address existing communicative needs and, in harnessing these technologies, people draw collaboratively on the semiotic resources made available by their individual trajectories, joint communicative purposes, physical and online spaces and wider sociocultural settings.
- As users become familiar with a new technology, they may start to reinterpret its affordances and thus to extend or alter their practices in ways that are shaped by their situated uses of the technology. As Kuijer et al. (2017: 21) put it, resourcefulness involves 'the adjusting of means to purpose, which inherently involves also adjusting purpose to means, up to the point where purpose becomes derived from means'. Through this process of social transformation, users may come to perceive the reconfigured and (re-)technologised (Jones and Hafner 2012) communicative practices as more or less normal, and the technology use becomes 'normalised' (Bax 2011).

In outlining this process, we downplay the novelty of digitally mediated communication carried out by mobile phone and focus on *continuities* in practice. Crucial to the concept of mobile resourcefulness is the extent to which use of new technologies is grounded in people's existing practices, problems and perceptions, sensitive to users' communicative and real-world purposes, and collaboratively conceived. In this way, the concept draws on the growing literature seeking to problematise the assumed dichotomy between offline and online worlds set up in early work on online interaction and communities (Turkle 1995) in order to show how technologies are embedded within multiple physical and social contexts (Cohen 2015; Lyons and Tagg 2019; Moores 2004) and the role they play in networked individuals' wider processes of (dis)identification (Leppänen et al. 2014). In emphasising continuity in practice rather than change, the concept speaks to a growing recognition of the importance of situating contemporary mediated practices within a wider chronological framework in order to trace developments in practice and provide historical points of comparison (Tagg and Evans 2020; and see Johnson 2011 for a history of diaries 'from Pepys to blogs'). This is not to deny the possibility of change or social transformation through new technology, but to see it as incremental and historically contingent. In particular, from a mobile resourcefulness perspective, social change emerges from people's perceptions of their present situation, and their attempts to address existing problems or practices through the adoption and adaptation of technologies.

Mobile Resourcefulness in Action

We end this chapter where we began, by reflecting on butcher Kang Chen's use of WeChat as a virtual noticeboard as a realisation of mobile resourcefulness, and then looking at two other examples of resourcefulness by Joanne and Winnie.

Kang's Virtual Noticeboard

Like many of our participants, Kang Chen relied increasingly on his mobile phone, and particularly WeChat, for running his business. Importantly, his mobile-enabled business model was not so much a planned innovation as a distributed response to a shifting complex of intersecting factors. Kang Chen initially downloaded WeChat towards the start of our data collection period, encouraged by his wife Meiyan, who was in turn urged by her brother-in-law in China to ensure her husband had access to the messaging app so they could maintain contact transnationally. His subsequent use of the app to receive and negotiate meat orders (the virtual noticeboard illustrated in Figure 3.1) emerged throughout 2014 as a convenient way to receive and record restaurant meat orders, given the perceived affordances of mobile messaging: asynchronicity, replicability and permanence, as well as the portability of the mobile phone which was always in Kang Chen's pocket. The practice was also enabled by credit arrangements which the butchers had with local restaurants, which meant the restaurants could order meat without having to arrange cash payments.

Previously, they had relied on discussing meat orders through voice calls or visiting in person, both of which they continued to do to a limited extent. However, messaging meat orders through WeChat made sense given the noise and bustle of the marketplace and the busy, hectic, mobile nature of Kang Chen's working day (and, he told us, that of his customers and suppliers). It meant they no longer had to carve out a shared time for interaction, but could fit their communications around their other daily activities. In their exchanges, the messages are framed not as conversational turns but as a kind of 'memo' or announcement that does not require a written response. Rather than a verbal reply, most orders elicit a physical action, that of preparing and sending the requested meat, which may take place hours or days after the message ('tomorrow' or 'Tuesday', Figure 3.1). Kang Chen does not need to respond immediately, and he can read the message when – and where – he likes. Kang Chen claimed not to have a routine but that he checked his phone whenever it suited him. His customers could easily leave a message for him to pick up by the end of the day, and he was aware that, in turn, he needed to have made a request to his suppliers (also by WeChat) by 9 pm in order to get a delivery the following day.

The remediation of meat ordering through WeChat is marked linguistically by a shift from the interpersonal register associated with conversational texting – featuring vague language and social formulae (Tagg 2012) – to a register characterised by precise linguistic choices and lexically dense noun phrases, as well as specialist lexis describing meat cuts. For example, one of Kang's turns in Figure 3.1 constitutes a lengthy noun phrase: '80 kg at 2 o'clock this afternoon after the new delivery or 50 kg to be delivered now?'. Furthermore, the messages are structured not as turns in an ongoing communication, but with formulaic openings and closings; in Figure 3.2, this involves the butcher stall name as salutation and the sign-off 'Many thanks'. This structural repetition may have been facilitated by the aforementioned affordance of cutting, pasting, manipulating and resending the text of previous messages. When Kang Chen breaks the routine to check an order he has forgotten (Figure 3.2), he indexes this shift in register with an informal 'hehe', drawing on the resources of more social texting to distance himself from the emergent mobile business register.

It was not long before Kang Chen would claim that he could not conduct his business without his mobile phone because he needed it to make and take orders. Far from exhibiting a radical break with pre-WeChat practices,

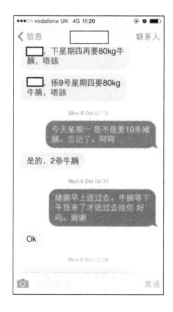

Figure 3.2 A shift in register on WeChat

however, this use of the messaging app is motivated by, and geared towards fulfilling, the butcher's long-term business and communicative goals, and shaped by contextual circumstances; that is, the messaging app serves to remediate his and his interactants' existing practices. At the same time, the technology shows signs of reshaping their practices, for example by removing the requirement or expectation to reply and prompting a concise, lexically dense register. It also, as previously noted, enabled assertions of identity that would not have been possible in spoken interactions, namely the fact that the interlocutors drew on two different but mutually intelligible scripts (the simplified script used in mainland China and the traditional one used in Hong Kong) indexing distinct cultural backgrounds.

The virtual noticeboard points to Kang Chen's agency in using WeChat for his own specific purposes in ways that make running his business more efficient and convenient. Such a conclusion fits the couple's wider narratives of becoming butchers in the UK, their stories of endurance and survival strategies, and the perception that they are particularly resourceful entrepreneurs; it also recognises that people are not simply passive users of technology designed by others. However, Kang Chen's agency in choosing to use WeChat in this way is socially situated and relational – it begins in the economic imperatives that brought him to the UK and is distributed across the various economic necessities, contextual demands, wider political and cultural forces, people, technologies, affordances and material artefacts involved in developing and shaping the mediated practice.

Joanne's WeChat Business

Like Kang Chen, WeChat was the only mobile phone app that Joanne, an adviser at the Chinese Community Centre (CCR) in Birmingham, used on a daily basis, with friends and family in China and the UK, as well as for work-related communication. One of Joanne's most frequent interlocutors during our data collection period was Zhao, a female family member living in China. The two combined interpersonal chat with discussion of their WeChat business. WeChat had introduced a new function called 'WeChat Store' (微店) whereby an e-business can be conducted through a reliable payment channel. Setting up and running digital stores is now a popular practice among WeChat users (Wang et al. 2020). Joanne and Zhao were early adopters of this commercial practice, identifying a niche market (powdered baby milk) and recognising and exploiting this affordance for their own purposes. They are arguably well placed to manage the business between them, with Joanne purchasing UK luxury goods while Zhao identifies customers in China. Importantly for our focus on mobile resourcefulness, they not only used WeChat to market products and collect money through the WeChat Store option, but they also used the chat function to negotiate and discuss the launch of their business. Figure 3.3 illustrates how Zhao and Joanne used WeChat to ascertain the viability of their WeChat business.

As with Kang Chen's noticeboard, their language choices contrast with typical text messages sent for social purposes which are generally characterised by vague language, playfulness and formulaic phrases (Tagg 2012). The precise yet compact language and noun phrases ('milk powder', 'average postage') again point to an emerging register of mobile business communication, which we also observed with other participants, such as Polish shop owner Edyta.

As shown in Figure 3.4a, the pair also exploited the functionality of taking photos with their mobile phones and embedding them into WeChat conversations to record and share with each other the availability and prices of products in the UK and China. The embedding of photos highlights the extent to which their WeChat conversations – and business – is deeply intertwined with offline activities taking place in physical contexts – chiefly the act of hunting out and pricing products in shops, as well as noticing products while window shopping. Figure 3.4a also shows how they drew fully on the range of resources available through WeChat, including voice messages.

Z:< I see>

J: < Milk powder costs 100 Yuan, the average postage will be 100 Yuan per can. If by air the goods will be received within 10 days. You will have to sell it at least 260 if you want to make a little profit. Would it be too expensive?>

Z: <900 grams per can>

Z: <postage is too expensive>

J: 900

Z: <wait for me to check the prices with the others who have done this business.>

Figure 3.3 Setting up a WeChat business

Their commercial activity also involves a network of contacts across the two countries, which Joanne and Zhao mobilise through WeChat. For example, in Figure 3.4a Zhao tells Joanne that she will check the prices with others engaged in a similar business, while in Figure 3.4b Joanne shares with Zhao pictures taken by her husband in Birmingham shops. As well as exploiting WeChat to set up an e-business, then, the pair also exploit it for its easy access to contacts they can call upon for help and efficient ways of sharing information. Their uptake of the app to conduct this business is prompted by the availability of WeChat Store, which was itself developed to capitalise on a growing need. It is also motivated by their awareness of the wider uptake around them, and made possible by their respective geographical locations and social networks. In choosing to take up this opportunity, the two friends are exerting their agency as networked individuals for personal gain.

Winnie's Learning

So far, we have looked at two instances in which mobile resourcefulness is bound up with commercial aims. Winnie's resourcefulness lies in the way she seeks to exploit elements of her shifting repertoire as opportunities not only to maintain different relationships and organise her social life, but to enact the values that hold true in her working, social and personal lives, and which are deeply situated in her cultural background, habitus and migratory history. Winnie, who was born in Hong Kong and migrated to the UK in

(a)

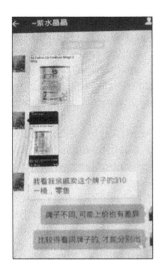

Z: [posts two photos of a can of milk powder]

Z: <I have asked one of my relatives who have been doing this business: 310 a can for this brand.>

J: < different brands might have different prices>

J: < have to check the same brand and compare their prices>

(b)

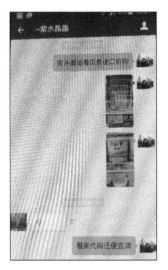

7/29/15 2:37AM

J: just saw there are foreign-branded formula milk on sale in those shops while I was window shopping

[J sends two pictures of canned formula-milk powder with price tags in Chinese]

7/29/15 8:39 AM

[Z sends a voice message]

J: It looks like our prices are cheaper

Figure 3.4a, b Pricing powdered milk through WeChat

1995, began working at the Library of Birmingham in 2000 as a Customer Experience Assistant. At the time of our data collection in 2015, she lived in Birmingham with her husband and had two grown-up children.

Like Kang, Winnie would probably not be described as an expert or prolific user of mobile phone communication or social media; she did not use social media sites such as Facebook or Instagram, and we noticed that she did not spend much time on her phone, perhaps because of other demands on her time as a working mother. At the time, she used an iPhone 4 passed down from her son. Many of her uses of SMS and WhatsApp might be described as that of micro-coordination, a use that Ling and Yttri (2002) identify as usually preceding a more emotional, interpersonal use. More accurately, Winnie negotiated interpersonal relationships and meanings while carrying out seemingly mundane social arrangements through her mobile phone.

Importantly, Winnie appeared to view mobile messaging as an informal space in which to practise and improve her English language skills (something she showed great concern for throughout our time with her), and to enact personal values which she often voiced in conversation with us and others, and which appeared to guide her behaviour at the library (Blackledge et al. 2016). These values, as documented by Blackledge et al. (2016), include politeness, independence – which manifested for Winnie in various ways, including evaluating and selecting from what she saw as Chinese and British ways of doing things (Lyons et al. 2020) – and the importance of learning, including English. In her mobile messaging, Winnie resourcefully marshalled all her English-language and other resources – both those previously acquired and those picked up in the course of messaging – in order to consolidate and maintain personal and family relationships and carry out various social roles, while navigating the challenges of the new platforms.

The following examples illustrate how new technologies become entangled in the co-construction of Winnie's social roles and relationships. Winnie performed her role of future mother-in-law to Aoife, her son's fiancé, through a careful selection of resources in WhatsApp.

> 29/03/2015 23:15: Aoife: Sorry I couldn't be at the meal Winnie. I wish you a safe flight to Hong Kong. I know this is going to be a difficult trip for you, I hope it is as peaceful as possible for you. Look after yourself. Thinking of you, see you when you get back. Lots of love, Aoife xxx
> 30/03/2015 11:47: Winnie: Thank you Aoife for your kind message and I hope you & Tom have a good time in Stockholm. Have a happy Easter love winnie
> 30/03/2015 11:51: Winnie: C u in 2 weeks time. ♥winnie

In her initiating message, Aoife apologises for missing a family meal, and sends her wishes ahead of Winnie's trip home to visit her mother, who was dying. The message appears respectful and polite, rather than intimate, full of the formulaic expression of interpersonal speech acts: *Sorry … I wish …*

I hope … Thinking of you. The message is less a conversational turn than a short letter, with salutation and sign-off (Baron 2000). Winnie adopts the same polite style, thanking Aoife for her comforting message and wishing the couple a good holiday and Easter. Her mobile messages were generally written with conventional spellings, and she consistently ended her sentences with full stops, a practice seen by younger texters as indexing negative feelings or an attempt to end the conversation (Busch 2021). Her formal style may have been co-constructed in interaction, as with Aoife, while her relatively novice status as a social media user may explain why Winnie adhered to conventions more traditionally associated with email or letters, rather than mobile messaging, such as the sign-off *love winnie* (arguably, a signature is not conventionally necessary in a mobile message and it is probably more common to sign off only with a kiss; Tagg 2012). Winnie was extending values she enacted offline – such as politeness and care in her written English – to her mobile interactions and thus remediating established practices through the new technology.

In China, it is generally taboo to address one's older relatives directly by their names or for older relatives to self-refer in that way, and it is likely that Winnie, with her awareness of Chinese traditions and customs, would appreciate this. This potentially invests the choice to use her first name in messages to her younger relative Aoife (*love winnie*) with greater pragmatic meaning than might otherwise be the case, signalling her attempt to reach out to Aoife. Our observations and interviews showed that Winnie was happy to be selective when adopting Chinese traditions, of which she was often suspicious (Blackledge et al. 2016: 29). For example, she rejected the traditionally authoritative mothering role typically valued in China and presented herself as a laid-back and open-minded parent (Blackledge et al. 2016: 27). This role is remediated through WhatsApp, as Winnie seeks to exploit the platform and its embedded resources to develop her relationship with her daughter-in-law.

In an apparent attempt to show her affection for Aoife and enhance their intimacy, Winnie also 'chunks' her message (Baron 2010), taking a follow-up turn in which she draws on a register which we might describe as 'txtspk' (Crystal 2001), which comprises letter homophones (*C u*) and emoji (♥). There is evidence elsewhere in her messages that Winnie was trying out respelt forms typically associated with digital communication and which she may have been learning from her seemingly more confident interactants; her friend Clare, for example, wrote in a much more consistently casual non-standard style than Winnie. As Shortis (2007) points out, respellings are typically learnt through interaction. In Figure 3.5, we can see an example of Winnie picking up a new abbreviation – and thus extending her repertoire – driven in this case by the need for understanding.

Figure 3.5 Extending a texting repertoire

When Clare suggests *Coffee 2mos* (meaning 'coffee tomorrow'), Winnie politely responds with *Nice to hear from you*, before asking for clarification of *mos*, which she understands indicates when they will meet: *What is mos mean? When?* Clare also uses *C u* and has a more informal, enthusiastic and less careful style than Winnie (*welcolm home!!*). Winnie does not copy Clare's style, but selectively accommodates to it, carefully expanding her repertoire of ways of writing in English.

In sum, Winnie's values are reflected in the social roles she enacted in her mobile messages; with Aoife, she performed the role of a laid-back, open-minded mother-in-law willing to lay aside Chinese traditions to show her affection. She was using WhatsApp resourcefully to pass on her personal values and extend her social role, and to try out new writing practices afforded by mobile messaging.

Conclusion

In this chapter, we laid out the concept of *mobile resourcefulness* as the socioculturally situated capacity to make the most of distributed semiotic resources associated with the mobile phone in accordance with contextual circumstances and towards some communicative or social end. Our argument is not that some uses of mobile phones are resourceful and others are not, but rather that people's mobile communication can best be understood in terms of their resourcefulness, and that their resourcefulness may manifest itself in diverse ways in different instances. The concept is intended to foreground the role of human endeavour and action in determining the uptake and use of mobile technologies, and has implications for understanding how spatial semiotic repertoires and their realisation at any one moment emerge from the complex interplay between habitus, individual trajectories and agency, on the one hand, and, on the other, the material constraints, cultural artefacts, wider discourses and interaction orders that inhabit, or flow through, the social space. At the same time, mobile resourcefulness is itself emergent and situated, and actions or decisions which may appear to be driven by an individual human agent can instead be conceptualised as the effect of an agency distributed across 'socially and historically constructed opportunities and obligations' (Miller, E.R. 2016: 359). In the following chapters (Chapters 4 and 5), we explore mobile resourcefulness further in relation to the media and semiotic resources made available by mobile messaging as part of people's broader repertoires.

4   Polymedia Repertoires

Introduction

In the afternoons, when Polish shopkeeper Edyta is in the shop and her 10-year-old daughter is home from school, the two keep in touch through their respective mobile devices: Edyta's mobile phone and Zuzanna's iPad and phone. They tend to use Polish, but much of their highly intimate and interpersonal communication involves sharing images and emoji, as illustrated in the extract from their Skype chat exchange in Figure 4.1 ('look mum' – *zobac[z] mamo*). They do not, however, see Skype, or SMS and Facebook Messenger as affording the same opportunities for non-verbal communication as the mobile messaging platform Viber, which provides access to 'stickers' – a broader, ever-growing range of pre-configured images. In the Skype exchange below, for example, Edyta directs their communication onto Viber: *ty jednak jestes Na viper sprawdz wyslalam Ci sticker* ('you're on Viber after all, check, I've sent you a sticker').

This chapter explores the relationship between resourcefulness and Madianou and Miller's (2012) theory of polymedia. In polymedia environments, an individual's communicative and social practices are not restricted to one social media platform, but involve drawing on affordances, combining different media, and movement between social media platforms like Skype and Viber. On one level, we argue that mobile phone users reach decisions about the appropriateness of a particular platform or app for a particular purpose by drawing on their mobile resourcefulness: the socioculturally situated capacity to make the most of distributed semiotic resources associated with the mobile phone in accordance with contextual circumstances and towards some communicative or social end. In this, navigating a polymedia environment also requires users to draw on their semiotic and media ideologies (Androutsopoulos 2021; Gershon 2010) – their beliefs regarding the particular communicative roles fulfilled by different platforms. On another level, we explore considerations of more complex

DOI: 10.4324/9780429031465-4

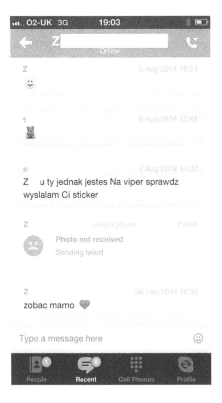

Figure 4.1 Moving from Skype to Viber

intersections of communicative resources at different levels of expression by drawing on our concept of the *polymedia repertoire* (Tagg and Lyons 2021) which recognises the full extent of semiotic resources available to individuals in making meaning.

The process of polymedia meaning-making is illustrated in this chapter through the example of Edyta, the Polish shop owner in London. We show that the mobile phone, and the platforms and apps accessed through it, are resources in people's polymedia repertoires that can be drawn upon in different ways as part of people's wider media ideologies and in pursuit of their communicative goals. The example shows how the deployment of people's polymedia repertoire is both motivated and shaped by individuals' mobile resourcefulness, which is itself deeply embedded in a complex of situational factors, including people's migratory trajectories, cultural backgrounds, social networks and communicative purposes.

The Polymedia Repertoire

As a theory of social media communication, polymedia has parallels with a number of other concepts, including media ecology (Ito et al. 2010), but its particular focus on how users exploit the affordances made available in the media environment makes it particularly relevant to our linguistic ethnographic approach. Polymedia conceptualises social media not in terms of distinct platforms but as an integrated communicative environment which users navigate in order to manage relationships and carry out social activities. As the range of social media platforms proliferate, each finds a niche in people's communicative repertoires depending on its affordances (Madianou 2015: 2) and, once barriers such as cost, access and media literacy skills recede, choice of platform becomes communicatively meaningful; in Madianou's (2014: 672) words, 'users are held responsible for their choices'. From a sociolinguistic perspective, polymedia thus opens up the possibility that platforms are meaningful communicative resources which, like linguistic resources, accrue particular social significance through usage which, in turn, shapes how individuals go on to use them. Like linguistic signs, platform choice is thus ideological, with site identities bound up with users' media ideologies and the uses they choose to make of them. Users' perception of the suitability of a media platform to accommodate their specific communicative needs within a framework of shared social conventions brings out the need for mobile resourcefulness in gauging how to exploit a particular platform – and when not to – as a significant aspect of contemporary interpersonal meaning-making.

In bringing together resourcefulness and polymedia, we thus draw on our notion of the *polymedia repertoire* (Tagg and Lyons 2021) which extends traditional ideas around the communicative repertoire by encompassing the full configuration of semiotic and technological resources accessed by networked individuals in the contemporary age. As suggested above, individuals in the current polymedia environment have access to a range of digital media which include devices (computers, laptops, tablets, phones), platforms (Instagram, Twitter) and channels of communication (for example, messaging or voice calls through a mobile messaging service). In principle, a polymedia repertoire includes non-digital media, such as the landline telephone, print media and television, although our focus in this chapter is primarily on digital communications technologies. Our argument is not simply that individuals use these technologies to communicate in particular ways – for example across large distances, asynchronously, and either for intimate chat or crowdsourcing – but that their media choices intersect with other communicative resources to make meaning in complex and non-arbitrary ways.

Our starting point is with communicative *practices* – what people want to achieve in the social world and the socially recognised and habitual ways in which these practices are carried out through particular genres, registers and styles. People's understandings of their socially situated practices shape the choices they make as to which devices, platforms, modes and signs they employ. Sending a work email through a mobile phone rather than a laptop, for example, may have implications for the way the software is accessed (its interface) and for the conditions in which the message is produced (an email may be written more concisely and sooner while the user is on the move) thus shaping how meanings are constructed and interpreted. A social media platform is similarly a resource into which other resources are embedded – including various communicative modes or channels – meaning that a poly-media repertoire takes the form of a *polymedia nest*, as shown in Figure 4.2, with, for example, semiotic signs such as emoji embedded into a particular platform, such as WhatsApp, which is in turn embedded into a mobile phone through which a particular platform is accessed. Polymedia nest embedding does not imply an inherent hierarchy between different types of resources, but a mutual interrelatedness between the layers of resources involved in the meaning-making process.

Linguistic and multimodal *signs* include those brought along by users – those associated with different language varieties, registers, styles, figurative devices, stance markers and so on – alongside those made available through particular apps or platforms. The latter include: typeface, font, layout, background design and colour (each of which may be offered to users as a set of choices or preconfigured); graphic and visual resources made available through the keypad, including punctuation and script (Androutsopoulos 2015); in-built functionalities such as the ability to design one's own profile and name groups; and sets of preconfigured graphicons such as emoji,

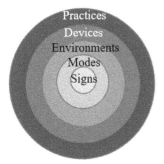

Figure 4.2 The polymedia nest (Tagg and Lyons 2021).

stickers and gifs. Polymedia thus draws attention to the multi-layered nature of the semiotic repertoire, as shown in Table 4.1. Users do not only choose signs from within each set – selecting one emoji rather than another or choosing its skin tone – but also move between predefined sets at the same level of expression, selecting a sticker, for example, if an appropriate emoji cannot be found; or inserting a gif rather than verbally describing a reaction (see Chapter 5). The use of these nested technological and semiotic resources is

Table 4.1 The polymedia repertoire (Tagg and Lyons 2021)

Polymedia repertoire layers		Definition	Examples
Practices		socially situated and habitual ways of doing things in the material and social world, shaped by knowledge of social genres and registers	networking with other organisations, keeping in touch with intimate others
Devices		physical objects with which users directly interact	mobile phone, tablet, laptop
Environments	Interface	the point where a user accesses and interacts with a platform	Facebook can be accessed through a web browser or a mobile phone app
	Platforms	sites which host and share content and allow for discussion, networking and feedback	social media sites Facebook and Instagram, and mobile messaging services WhatsApp, Viber, WeChat
	Channels	various communication modes often integrated into a platform	voice calls, private messages, group chats, wall posts or status updates
Modes		different ways in which a message can be represented	speech, writing and visual communication (which can in turn be broken down into different modal resources)
Signs		elements of linguistic and modal systems which convey symbolic, indexical and iconic meaning	words, set phrases, emoji and other pre-configured signs

shaped in the first instance by people's practices – by what they are trying to achieve through these resources in the material social world.

As semiotic resources, platforms such as Facebook or WhatsApp enable meaning-making through a complex dialectic relationship between the platform itself and layered meaning-making resources forming part of the polymedia repertoire. On the one hand, platforms establish what Djonov and van Leeuwen (2018) call a 'built-in semiotic regime' by which certain embedded resources are made more visible and accessible than others, with their use and meaning potential regulated through menus, commands and prompts. On the other hand, the ways in which these resources are selected and deployed by users within a particular platform are driven also by wider semiotic and social practices, discourses and ideologies, and shaped by individuals' immediate and long-term communicative goals. The effect of these processes is twofold: the use of embedded resources not only shapes how a platform or device is perceived and what its social significance is in the polymedia environment, but the platform in turn has the potential to shape the communicative significance of the embedded resources.

The polymedia repertoire enables us to explore how our participants' mobile resourcefulness – their situated capacity to exploit their mobile phone to achieve social goals – is realised in interactional encounters through selecting between, integrating and deploying different levels of expression. In the next section, we show how Edyta used elements of her polymedia repertoire to negotiate various social relationships and to remediate and extend her everyday business transactions. The discussion of her mediated business practices also draws attention to the fact that 'being resourceful' in one's use of the mobile phone is far from unproblematic or straightforward, but involves rubbing up against and negotiating other people's aims and expectations, and often engaging in unwanted or unhelpful interactions.

Edyta's Polymedia Repertoire at Work

Practices

At the time of our data collection in late 2014 and early 2015, Edyta's polymedia repertoire was shaped by her intertwined personal and business-related practices. These were in turn shaped by her wider social context which centred around the Polish shop in the East London borough of Newham which she ran with her husband, Tadeusz, and in which she spent much of her time. Our observations and interviews suggest that the couple, like Kang Chen and Meiyan Chew, had an entrepreneurial spirit – what we might call 'entrepreneurial resourcefulness'. They originally planned to stay in the UK for a few years, save some money and return to Poland. Like many other Polish migrants

Figure 4.3 Edyta and Taduesz's polski sklep

in the UK (and no doubt responding to the wider socio-economic and political context), a few years later the couple decided to stay and look for ways in which they could make more money and work for themselves. Over the next few years, they used their savings to open three shops in East London, the last being the one in Newham (open from 2007 to 2015) where we carried out our research (Figure 4.3). In separate interviews, both Edyta and her husband constructed narratives of personal struggle and determination, marked by their ability to identify and seize opportunities (Zhu Hua et al. 2015). According to their narrative, they worked hard to buy the shops; as Tadeusz said,

> 'sklep założyliśmy w 2005 roku ale z pomysłem już nosiliśmy się od jakichś trzech czterech lat tylko po prostu nie mo- nie mieliśmy jeszcze funduszy na to i robiliśmy po prostu wszystko żeby zaoszczędzić jakieś pieniądze'
>
> *we opened the [first] shop in 2005 but we had been thinking about it for about three or four years but we just didn't have the funds for it and we were doing simply everything to save some money*
>
> (Tadeusz, interview)

Their idea to open a shop was driven by the desire to work for themselves and emanated from their perception of the need for Polish shops in East London:

> 'przeprowadziliśmy sie w tą stronę um Londynu um i przeszkadzało nam to że nie ma tutaj polskiego sklepu i zauważyliśmy że jest takie

zapotrzebowanie bo jest dużo Polaków i że może spróbujemy w tym um w tym zakresie coś zrobić'
we moved to this part of um London um and we didn't like the fact there wasn't a Polish shop here and we noticed that there is a demand because there were a lot of Polish people and that maybe we would try to do something in this area
(Edyta, interview)

As Edyta pointed out in interview, 'początki były ciężkie' ('the beginnings were tough'), and the couple learnt how to run the business on the job. Both Tadeusz and Edyta emphasise the fact that they did a lot by themselves, including furnishing the shop and learning how to work the equipment; as Edyta said of using the till, 'uczyliśmy się sami na podstawie instrukcji' ('we were learning by ourselves from the manual'). The couple appeared to value their own resourcefulness over reliance on others:

'sami wszystko organizowaliśmy po prostu no bo jakoś tak nie lubimy chodzić pytać się no wypadałoby pojechać do sklepu na Hammersmith zapukać i (knocks on the till twice) a powiedzcie nam gdzie towar kupić (…) ale my nie my po prostu sami lubimy um takie rzeczy organizujemy'
we organised everything by ourselves simply because we don't like asking around well we could have gone to a shop in Hammersmith knock and (Tadeusz knocks on the till twice) tell us where to buy goods (…) but we don't we simply like to organise um these things ourselves
(Tadeusz, interview)

Their narrative recounts their initial success, and then a decline in business due to increasing competition. Although the couple were to eventually sell the shop, at the time of our interviews, they had identified gaps in the current market and outlined possible future opportunities:

'jeśli ktoś by tutaj otworzył coś podobnego ale zaangażował się jeszcze wiesz coś roz- roz- rozkręcił to wiesz jakieś pomysły są różne można robić kurczaki świeże bułeczki czy jakąś minikafejkę tam bo miejsca jest dużo gdyby się chciało można z tego jeszcze zrobić coś'
if someone was to open something similar here but put their heart into it it could still work you know there are different ideas you can do chickens fresh bread rolls or some kind of mini café because there is a lot of space if you wanted to you could make something out of it
(Edyta, interview)

As their background story suggests, Edyta's and her husband's entrepreneurism was grounded in a resourcefulness deeply embedded in their lived experience and situated awareness of the immediate context. This resourcefulness was also evident in the transactional encounters that took place in the shop. As noted in our fieldnotes, the specialised nature of the shop and its symbolic marking as a Polish space – Edyta claimed in interview that *90% produktów to są produkty polskie (90% of the products are Polish)* – resulted in a limited number of interactions with people and businesses outside the targeted customer group of Polish and Eastern European people (Zhu Hua et al. 2015). This led to the prevalence of the Polish language in business transactions, which in turn discouraged Edyta from pursuing English-language lessons. We observed Edyta's English to be 'limited in vocabulary' but 'functional' (Zhu Hua et al. 2015: 14). Despite the couple's stated preference for Polish, however, our observations and recordings revealed a range of semiotic resources in play, including English and Russian, which Edyta had learned at school but claimed to have forgotten. See, for example, the exchange below between Edyta (E) and a Russian-speaking customer (C).

C	Здравствуйте!	**Hello!**
E	Здравствуйте!	**Hello!**
C	Мне нужно у вас (inaudible) Tak. Ну	**I need you** (inaudible). Yes. Let's
E	дaвaй кусочек (11) tego. (sound of	**have a piece of** (11) this. (sound
C	till)	of till)
E	Którą?	Which one?
C	Tego.	This one.
E	Tą?	This?
C	Może {tak tez bo to tak} (?)	Maybe {like this because it's so} (?)
E	Też taki sam кусочек?	Also **a piece** like that?
E	Ehh дa po/пo кусочку tak tak.	Uh **yes a piece** each yes yes.
C	Dobra. (12, sound of till)	Ok. (12, sound of till)
E	Uhum. (sound of till)	Uhum. (sound of till)
C	I/И здесь takiego мясочка кусочек.	And here a piece of this meat.
E	Tego?	This one?
C	Tak. Tego. Tego.	Yes. This one. This one.
	(laughing) Boczek. Bacon.	(laughing) Bacon. *Bacon.*
	Bacon. Tak. Bacon.	*Bacon.* Yes. *Bacon.*

[Note: in the translation, Russian original is represented in **bold**, English in *italics*, Polish in regular script and ambiguous language is underlined. Words in { } represent researcher's best guess; the length of pauses between utterances are indicated in number.]

Devices

In line with our impression of our other participants (see Chapter 1), Edyta's polymedia repertoire was dominated in terms of devices by the mobile phone. At the time of our research, Edyta had a mobile phone contract with inclusive data transfer allowance on an iPhone. Her husband also owned an iPhone on a contract. Zuzanna, Edyta and Tadeusz's 10-year-old daughter owned an iPad, which she used to communicate, watch videos and read. At the time of our data collection, it was Edyta rather than Tadeusz who used mobile messaging for business-related purposes. In fact, Edyta used her iPhone extensively both at work and at home, for both business and private purposes.

Within this wider polymedia context, Edyta's use of her mobile phone with customers and suppliers can best be understood with reference to the concept of mobile resourcefulness; that is, as the socioculturally situated capacity to make the most of distributed semiotic resources associated with the mobile phone in accordance with contextual circumstances and towards some communicative or social end. The couple originally used the shop's landline to contact suppliers and customers but, according to Edyta, when the phone broke, she started to use her personal mobile phone for business purposes instead of buying a new phone, effecting a shift in the communicative niches held by different devices in her polymedia repertoire. This shift resembles Kang Chen's gradual move from voice calls and in-person visits towards WeChat for taking restaurant orders, and can similarly be seen as an individual appropriation of technology, which nonetheless is likely to have been partly inspired by a more general shift in the way we use technology and its progressive development. The agency, then, is situated and relational and shaped by contextual circumstances. Edyta explained that using her phone just felt natural. She elaborated on the convenience of SMS over voice calls, not only for her but for her suppliers.

'E: często wysyłam zamówienia mailem (.) korespondencję um smsową prowadzę z dostawcami
A: czemu nie telefoniczną
E: um ponieważ jest to wygodniejsze (.) i dla mnie i dla na przykład dostawc[y] który w tym czasie może prowadzić samochód albo przyjmuje zamówienie w innym sklepie jest dla niego niezręcznie odbierać um telefon więc umówiliśmy się że w ten sposób się będziemy um komunikować'
E: *I often place orders by email (.) and communicate with suppliers by text-messages*
A: *why don't you call*
E: *um because it's more convenient (.) both for me and for example for a supplier who might be driving or taking an order in another shop at the time and it's awkward for him to answer um the phone so we've agreed that we would communicate in this way*

                                                             (Edyta, interview)

The decision to carry out business practices by mobile messaging, then, was made relevant by the communicative gap left by the breaking of the old technology, and shaped by the demands and constraints of working lives. It also emerged from Edyta's habitus: the existing role of the mobile phone in her communicative practices, which made it a 'natural' substitute – we noted that Edyta carried her phone everywhere and was almost constantly potentially available; on one occasion, she was using her phone at the counter and barely looked up from it to serve a customer (the incident is recorded in Zhu Hua et al. 2017). In this sense, this shift in her polymedia repertoire – the uptake of her mobile phone for business-related exchanges – shows mobile resourcefulness, the ability to recognise and exploit elements of her polymedia repertoire in contextually relevant ways in order to address her communicative needs.

Environments

There was little sign that Edyta was either an extensive or strategic user of social media. Their Polish shop had a negligible online presence. The fact that they did not promote their business online no doubt reflects their local customer base but also mirrors their limited personal use of social media sites like Facebook: although Edyta posted photos on Facebook, when asked about some of the posts on her Facebook wall, she was not aware they were there. In contrast, she was a frequent user of the mobile messaging apps Viber, Facebook Messenger and SMS text messaging, which she used for a range of purposes, including to keep in touch with friends in Poland, liaise with her husband and daughter throughout the day, and maintain contact with customers and suppliers, usually in one-to-one interactions rather than groups.

An individual's choice of app at any one time rests on their awareness of the affordances associated with each, and is potentially communicatively meaningful (Madianou and Miller 2012). Edyta tended to use the free internet-enabled messaging app Viber for personal communication with her daughter and friends not only because of their easy access to mobile data but also the availability of virtual stickers with the app (see Chapter 5 and, e.g., Tang and Hew 2019). The vast majority of her Viber exchanges – mostly sent from the shop – include stickers, and they appear to both reflect and construct close, friendly and informal relationships. For example, while working Edyta keeps in touch with A., her friend in Poland, and their light-hearted banter (see Figure 4.4) constitutes a personal communicative dimension oriented towards the professional context of the shop (A. asks *Co porabiasz w sklepie je[s]tes* 'What are you up to are you at the shop'), but is not primarily associated with the transactional communicative activities that characterise the shop. Instead, the conversation in Figure 4.4 centres on the mundane topic of eating,

What are you up to are you at the
shop

Yes and I could eat something

Eat then

[visual]

I know I know golly I'm just
eating

I'm already full up and now I'm
drinking (xxx) eat

Figure 4.4 Chatting on Viber while at work.

which serves as a means by which to keep the channel of communication
open. This is evident in lexical patterning as the two interlocutors respond
closely to each other's lexical choices, engaging in what Tannen (1989)
calls 'repetition with variation': *jesc mi sie chce* ('I could eat something'),
To jedz ('Eat then'), *Jem kurcze* ('I'm just eating'), *Ja juz sie najadlam*
('I'm already full up'). On the one hand, such repetition displays participatory listenership (Tannen 1989: 59) – it shows that the interlocutors are
paying attention to what is being said. On the other hand, it points to the
primarily phatic nature of the interaction, with the pair focused on the
form of each other's utterances rather than engaging deeply in the topic,
or with each other. While originally discussed in relation to spoken interactions by Tannen, such displays of attention may be particularly important to mobile conversations in which social presence must be constructed
through textual or graphical means (see also Chapter 5).

The sticker in this exchange – and others in the dataset – has a primarily
interpersonal purpose. In this case, the information load is carried by the

verbal text (e.g., *To jedz*, 'eat then') while the sticker appears to be carefully chosen to both reflect the message content and suggest a light-hearted take. As with the linguistic aspects of the message, the lack of informational load, and the clever but sometimes random connections made, suggest a primarily playful use intended to amuse or entertain rather than suggesting more serious engagement with what the other is saying. This playful use of stickers likely contributed to Edyta and her interlocutors' perception of Viber as an interpersonal, playful and intimate space, which in turn shaped how the stickers were interpreted.

Edyta also punctuates her working day with Viber messages to her daughter, usually in the afternoon when Zuzanna is at home. The messages in Figure 4.5 were sent while Zuzanna was at home unwell.

In this case, Edyta uses stickers not so much to amuse but to convey her sympathy and concern over her daughter's health. The image of the sick boy in bed appears to index Edyta's appreciation of her daughter's poorly state. In the case of the mug of coffee and chocolate cake stickers in Figure 4.5,

How are you feeling darling? Shall I bring you anything?

How are things, Zuzanna? Is Daddy home yet?

Figure 4.5 Checking up on children through Viber while at work.

the precise semantic meaning of the sticker appears less relevant than the pragmatic function of showing attention and care through sharing. At the same time, Edyta also uses stickers to encourage her daughter to reply in a way that may seem less demanding than verbal writing – the command does not come directly from Edyta but is delivered within a playful framing suggested by the visual joke in the sticker (the Viber message being sent in the post). It is also written in a language, English, which Zuzanna would not typically associate with her mother.

Interactions with suppliers and customers were carried out by Facebook Messenger or by SMS. The choice of Facebook Messenger for interacting with customers can be explained by the fact that it did not require customers to know Edyta's private phone number as they connected with her through the 'semi-public' social network site. We might argue that these factors and the communicative practices associated with each app may have led to Facebook Messenger and SMS being seen by Edyta and her interlocutors as less intimate than other apps like Viber, which they associated with more informal and playful communication. This distinction is reflected in studies suggesting that SMS might be used less 'conversationally' than internet-enabled apps such as WhatsApp (or Viber) because the perceived cost of sending an SMS – as well as engrained habit – can mean that users construct longer messages rather than taking rapid shorter and more frequent turns (see Chapter 1; Church and de Oliveira 2013; König 2019). Through habitual uses, these different apps may thus come to fill particular communicative niches in these interlocutors' semiotic repertoires.

Modes and Signs

Suppliers: Organising Deliveries by SMS

In this example of her mobile messaging interactions with suppliers (Figure 4.6), Edyta contacts her sales representative to request an update and enquire about additional items she had ordered (*slaska* and *glogowska*, two types of sausage; and *uszka*, traditional small dumplings). The exchange highlights how the two interlocutors draw resourcefully on SMS and its affordances in order to carry out this task. The 'micro-coordination' of everyday social activities has long been recognised as a common use of SMS (Ling and Yttri 2002); here, the practice is extended to fulfil a business function.

The particular register adopted by these interlocutors emerges from their commercial goals, the nature of their relationship, and the wider sociocultural context. The register is realised through the use of linguistic signs

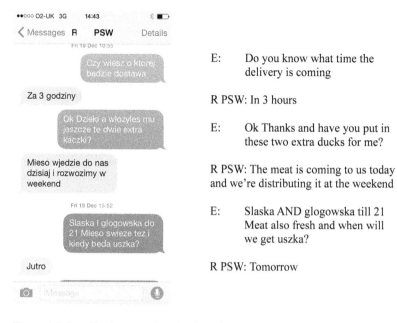

Figure 4.6 Coordinating a stock order through SMS

from the interlocutors' overlapping repertoires. The resources include specialist Polish lexis and noun phrases relating to their trade ('Slaska AND glogowska') and enable brevity and speed: the lack of time stamps suggests that the turns are rapid and the interlocutors orient towards an immediate (or near future) time: 'In 3 hours', 'today', 'tomorrow', while grammatical ellipsis (e.g., *Za 3 godziny*) and the omission of openings and closings enable both parties to focus on pursuit of immediate goals. The linguistic and typographic resources (unconventional punctuation, grammatical ellipsis, omission of diacritics, and informal expressions like 'Ok') depart from those generally upheld in more highly regulated writing spaces. Interestingly, the capitalisation of AND in 'Slaska AND glogowska' (*Slaska I glogowska*) was likely caused by the default setting of the English keyboard which capitalises all lower case *i*'s, and thus constitutes an incidental use of a resource. English-related lexis like 'Ok' and 'weekend' in this exchange are often borrowed into informal Polish, although here it can also be seen to index their identities as Poles in London who have 'made this English language Polish a bit', as Tadeusz said in interview. He added that it was now easier for him to use certain English words like 'invoice' than the Polish equivalents. Finally, the interlocutors employ informal grammatical resources which transgress the established politeness norms that might be expected in customer-supplier exchanges in Poland. For example, Edyta addresses the supplier using familiar second-person singular verb forms, rather than the polite second-person pronouns *Pan/Pani* followed by verbs in third-person singular, used as standard among adult Polish speakers whose relationship is not very close (as in this case): *wiesz* rather than *pan wie* ('you know'), and *wlozyles* rather than *pan wlozyl* ('you put in'). This informal business register is emergent in that it is co-created in the course of unfolding interactions, and its co-creation is *resourceful* in the sense that users draw both on their wider semiotic repertoires and the affordances of the mobile app in maintaining a social relationship and efficiently pursuing business-related communicative goals.

The use of familiar verb forms is likely facilitated as much by the English-language context where the distinction between polite and familiar pronoun forms does not exist, as by the medium and its propensity for heightening intimacy and blurring boundaries between business and personal contexts. It seems this informality reflected the nature of the couple's wider relationships with the suppliers. Face-to-face interactions between the shop owners and their suppliers (when we observed the latter visiting the shop) were similarly informal and relaxed. The use of mobile messaging served to remediate existing practices, roles and relationships which had once been carried out over the landline and were still also carried out face-to-face.

Customers: Pre-ordering and Stock Checking

As well as suppliers, customers often contacted Edyta through mobile messaging to pre-order items or to check stock availability, initially through landline or voice calls, and increasingly through either Facebook Messenger or SMS. This practice was beneficial to both parties: it ensured that the customer got the required product and that the couple would make a sale. Tadeusz told us in interview:

'jak ktoś się na przykład chce zapytać czy ma w sklepie to a to no to puści jej tam um zapytanie na Fejsie albo też ma numery powymieniane z wieloma ludźmi więc smsami też się pytają (...) wiesz że przed świętami mieliśmy karpie no to ludzie tacy co już na przykład tu nie mieszkają ale kiedyś robili u nas zakupy to wysyłali jej smsa zostaw mi karpia bo przyjadę bo u ciebie chcę kupić bo akurat już wiedzą że tu są dobre że my zawsze dobre mieliśmy te ryby'

> *if someone wants to ask for example whether this or that is available in the shop they send her [Edyta] a question on Facebook or she has also exchanged numbers with many people so they ask through text-messages as well (...) you know we had carp before Christmas so people who don't live here anymore but did their shopping here in the past sent her a text save some carp for me because I will come because I want to buy from you because they know that we've got good ones that we've always had good fish*
>
> (Tadeusz, interview)

Edyta's decision to use mobile messaging with her customers can be described as distributed: she told us that the practice was initiated by customers who would find her on Facebook, and that she started giving them her private number when their landline at the shop broke; in fact, her phrase *tak to wychodziło wszystko* ('that's how it worked out') appears to deny any individual agency.

'E: klienci to wyszło od klientów (…) bo zaczęli do mnie pisać więc um
A: znaleźli cię na przykład na Facebooku czy jakoś tak czy jak to
E: często prosili o numer telefonu na przykład a mi się zepsuł ten numer (…) wtedy podawałam prywatny i tak to wychodziło wszystko'
E: *customers it was initiated by customers (...) because they started writing to me so um*
A: *did they find you for example on Facebook or something like that or how*
E: *they often asked for the phone number for example and this number has broken (...) then I would give my private one and that's how it worked out*

(Edyta, interview)

The fact that Edyta accepted customers as Friends on Facebook or shared her personal contact details with them is perhaps not surprising, not only because the shop acted as a sociocultural hub among the local Polish community but also given the close and friendly relationships that the couple enjoyed – in fact, actively fostered – with their customers. In her fieldnotes, Agnieszka notes her conversation with Edyta on this.

> I asked Edyta about her contact with her customers … She said that she was friendly to them and tried to get to know them. She said they told her more than when they go to confession and she would have a lot to gossip about. I asked why she thought people were so open with

her and she said that she didn't think it had anything to do with her specifically, but that 'Polak potrzebuje się wygadać'. [A Pole needs to offload.]

(AL, 5/9/14)

The decision for Edyta and her customers to communicate by mobile messaging is also shaped by the nature of their work and the affordances of mobile messaging in comparison to, for example, mobile voice calls. In Figure 4.7, a customer who is Friends with Edyta on Facebook contacts her through Facebook Messenger on 23rd December to check on the availability of *żubrówka* (bison grass vodka). The portability of the mobile phone means that he can – or must – use it to first ascertain her location (*Jestes dzis w sklepie?*, 'Are you at the shop today?'), with the act of establishing location itself a potential resource in prefacing his request (cf. Arminen 2006; Laursen and Szymanski 2013; Lyons and Ounoughi 2020). The affordance of immediacy associated with mobile messaging underlies his request and

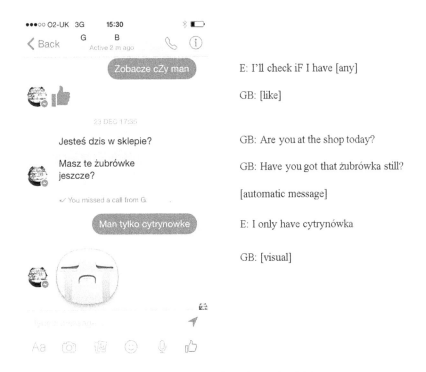

Figure 4.7 Checking product availability through Facebook Messenger

motivates his subsequent call (either because Edyta does not immediately reply or because he can see from the app that she is not 'active'; i.e., doesn't have FB Messenger open). Edyta either cannot pick up (because she is serving a customer or dealing with stock) or she chooses not to, perhaps because she sees little business opportunity in discussing a produce she does not have. In either case, her subsequent choice of the written channel is communicatively significant in indexing the nature and status of the exchange and the kind of social relationship being performed – and provides the customer with time and space to contemplate the alternative product suggested by Edyta.

What may seem important to Edyta about Facebook Messenger as a means to this particular end is that it can be quick: again, conversations are marked by brief turns with no extended openings and closings, and resources such as Likes and emoji – which are both communicatively efficient and interpersonally important – are made available. The key role of such multimodal resources is evident in Figure 4.7. In response to the customer's query about *żubrówka* (bison grass vodka), Edyta reports that she only has *cytrynówka* (lemon-flavoured vodka), thus saving the customer a wasted journey. The customer responds with an emoji of a crying face which efficiently serves to acknowledge receipt of the message and convey their disappointment, whilst not inviting further discussion. By exploiting the availability of emoji in this digital space, the customer also maintains an intimate and playful register and thus avoids losing face by turning down the alternative product suggested by Edyta. A similar point can be made about the Like posted by the same customer in response to Edyta's offer to check availability of the product (*Zobacze cZy man*). In both cases, the multimodal resources serve to indicate an appropriate response – an acknowledgement of Edyta's message – in a way that is expressive and engaging, without making further demands on Edyta's time.

Another example of stock checking via FB Messenger can be seen in Figure 4.8. In this case, Edyta draws on her phone's camera function – and the capacity to send photos via FB Messenger – to take a photo in the shop in order to facilitate the business transaction by providing the customer with a momentary 'window' onto the shop. The exchange has been initiated by the customer and shaped by Edyta's uncertainty over the intended product. The choice of resources here again suggests business-like intimacy, and the use of Facebook Messenger means the exchange can be done quickly and in their own time. These examples highlight the situated resourcefulness evident in the use of mobile messaging for the purpose of ensuring successful transactions, and the ways in which existing business practices and relationships are shaped through remediation.

E:	[photo of a magazine in the shop]
E:	Is it This newspaper
D:	[bouncing grinning emoji]
D:	Yes thanks I'll come to get it tomorrow

Figure 4.8 Pre-ordering shop items through Facebook Messenger

The Mobile Phone as a Double-Edged Sword

By the time of our fieldwork, Edyta was noticeably tiring of the shop. She described her long days in the shop as *prozaicznie* ('mundane'), a statement borne out by the time she spent there by herself (or with our research fellow), and she was not interested in following up on any of the couple's potential aspirations for the future of the shop (and, indeed, they were to go on and sell it after our fieldwork). We saw evidence of her boredom in Viber messages sent to friends (based in Poland) from the shop. In Figure 4.9, she shares that she was crying uncontrollably (*wylam*) out of boredom earlier that day.

Her emergent mobile contact with customers may have played a small part in her growing frustration, by contributing to the perhaps inevitable intrusion of her work life into private spaces (see Papacharissi 2011 on the convergence of spheres of life through the mobile phone). For Edyta and Tadeusz as co-owners of a family business, the boundaries between work and home life were blurred (Tagg and Lyons 2017). As mentioned earlier, we observed that Edyta carried her phone everywhere and was almost constantly potentially available, including for those of her customers who had her mobile phone number. The sense of being 'always on' is linked elsewhere to increased stress in the workplace (Maier and Deluliis 2015; Reinsch et al. 2008) and Edyta recognised it as interfering with her family life. In her words,

'już zaczyna mi przeszkadzać bo jednak co chwilę (…) jestem gdzieś tam z Zuzanną dajmy na to a ktoś mi pisze "zamów mi tort bo muszę

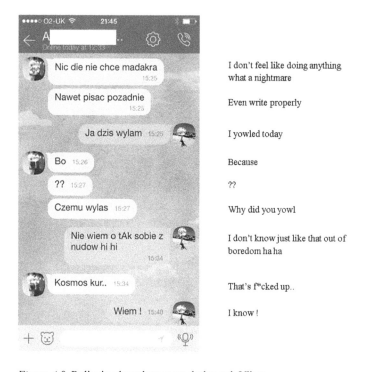

Figure 4.9 Relieving boredom at work through Viber

mieć go na jutro" więc ja wiesz w trakcie jakiegoś assembly szkolnego Zuzanny muszę gdzieśtam pisać dzwonić pomimo tego że nie jestem w pracy w tym czasie bo czuję się zobowiazana w stosunku do klienta'

> *it's starting to bother me already because often (...) I'm somewhere with Zuzanna for example and someone is writing to me 'order a cake for me because I have to have it for tomorrow' so you know during say Zuzanna's school assembly I have to write or phone somewhere despite the fact that I'm not at work at that time because I feel obliged towards the customer*

(Edyta, interview)

An indication of Edyta's growing frustration with this element of her working life is shown in this last example (Figure 4.10), where a customer (Marek) asks her for Viagra (see Lyons and Tagg 2019 for extended discussion of this exchange).

The exchange is grounded in the customer's familiarity with the practice of pre-ordering stock, and involves a renegotiation of the boundaries of this practice. Both interlocutors draw resourcefully on their shared repertoire in handling this potentially communicatively awkward social encounter. Marek initially draws on the somewhat formal business register typical of such requests in our dataset ('Have you got the possibility to arrange'), but the lack of response from Edyta prompts him to switch to a more informal register ('Where have you disappeared to?'). Edyta's frustration with this request is initially indicated in a playful fashion – namely by referring to a well-known Polish joke about using a glass of water as a contraceptive method – to index a shared background and mitigate the unwelcome request. Marek acknowledges the shared reference ('We're familiar with this response') and then appears to distance himself from his request, first explaining it and then changing the subject in a way that indexes a wider personal relationship: 'When are we going for a drink?', a suggestion that might be read as another trespass on Edyta's personal boundaries. Edyta's final message in Figure 4.10 responds to Marek's suggestion that she might have access to Viagra in a way

M: Hi Edyta.Have you got the possibility to arrange normal blue Viagra from Poland ?M

M: Where have you disappeared to?let me know about the tablets because man needs them

E: 'man' should have a glass of water instead if he can't!

M: We're familiar with this response.I thought you had access but if not then ok.

M: When are we going for a drink?

E: No I don't have access what am I a chemist or something ? How are things with you?

Figure 4.10 Negotiating the boundaries of the customer–shop owner relationship.

that makes explicit her frustration: *a co to ja chemik czy co?* ('what am I a chemist or something?'). The remediation of business relationships through the intimate space of the mobile messaging app was having implications that went beyond Edyta's work-related practices. The fact that technology is often a double-edged sword bringing both benefits and unwanted outcomes (e.g., Ling and Horst 2011) points to the complexities and uncertainties of a distributed mobile resourcefulness shaped by multiple interests and circumstances.

Conclusion

In this chapter, we drew on the case of Edyta, a Polish shop owner in London, to explore how mobile resourcefulness motivates and shapes people's deployment of multilayered polymedia repertoires in the contexts of their wider social practices, beliefs and purposes.

Edyta's polymedia repertoire centred around her mobile phone, which she used in the shop (and elsewhere) to carry out a range of intersecting social and business activities. Her polymedia repertoire was structured by audience and purpose, with certain mobile messaging apps used with friends and family, and others with suppliers and customers at work. Her resourcefulness is particularly evident in the way she remediated many of her business practices through mobile messaging, an action which emerged from the broken landline and which served to fulfil existing communicative needs. It met the demands of her and her business partners' working lives, drew on the affordances of the mobile phone, and was influenced by Edyta's habitus, the habit of keeping her phone always with her. In these emergent social spaces, Edyta and her interlocutors co-construct a shared polymedia repertoire which includes resources made available by the technology (stickers, Likes, emoji, photos), those sanctioned in contrasting ways by the expectations of the mobile space (informal expressions, grammatical ellipsis, omitted diacritics and so on) and by the interactants' orientation towards Polish standard language norms. It also includes resources associated with the multiple social contexts in which they are situated (Polish business terms, English-associated resources). The use of mobile messaging did not effect any great transformation in Edyta's business practices, but their remediation through this new technology brought more gradual change. It provided a written record of supplies that Edyta could respond to in her own time (similar to Kang's virtual noticeboard), reconfigured her relationships with customers, and further blurred the perceived boundaries between her working and private life. These changes were not necessarily intended and were not always perceived as desirable, with Edyta beginning to resent the way in which her emerging polymedia repertoire enabled customers to contact her at any time.

The notion of the polymedia repertoire adds to our understanding of mobile resourcefulness by highlighting the multilayered nature of individual repertoires, comprising a range of devices, platforms and channels alongside semiotic modes and signs. Resourcefulness thus involves not only the selection of resources but also their combination and intersection in contextually appropriate ways. In the next chapter, we focus on the range of linguistic and multimodal signs that are embedded into mobile phone messaging apps, and explore the ways in which people resourcefully exploit these in grabbing and managing their friends' attention in the busy polymedia environment.

5   Sharing in Mobile Conversations

Introduction

In his friends' WhatsApp group chat, Hong Kong-born salon manager Joe posts a link to a video on Facebook (Figure 5.1). He does not use verbal text to either direct his friends' attention to it or demand a response; instead, he presents it for their attention. In this case, Grace and Sally quickly respond with exaggerated displays of enthusiasm indicated through the expression *Omg* ('oh my god') and punctuation and emoji flooding. The act of sharing a link is an accepted and welcome practice in the group and it appears to fulfil primarily interpersonal functions of reaching out, entertaining each other and bonding.

In this chapter, we analyse our participants' conversations via mobile messaging apps. We draw on interactional sociolinguistics and (digital) conversation analysis approaches to detail how acts of sharing serve to remediate interpersonal relationships, providing space for individual agency and autonomy as well as facilitating face-saving for both the posters and their

Figure 5.1 Sharing a weblink on WhatsApp

DOI: 10.4324/9780429031465-5

interlocutors. In our data, such acts of sharing often rely on an assumption of common contextual knowledge: in-group knowledge and shared interactional histories, which means that shared content does not require an explanation. This process can in turn heighten the sense of intimacy between interlocutors, while at the same time enabling each group member to engage and disengage with the shared content in line with their contexts and circumstances. In the case of personal images or 'homemade' videos, sharing also invites greater familiarity by giving people a peek into their interlocutors' immediate physical contexts. The enthused linguistic and multimodal responses, like those in Figure 5.1, are typical of those given across closed WhatsApp groups in our data, although in some cases acts of sharing also open up spaces for negotiation, contestation and (sometimes) misunderstanding.

In the chapter, we explore the above-raised points and argue that acts of sharing and appreciation can be understood in terms of mobile resourcefulness, in that people are drawing on the available digital resources in creating new ritualised practices through which offline friendships are remediated and reshaped. We unpack the polymedia nest, focusing on how emoji and other multimodal resources are embedded in mobile messaging platforms on mobile devices, and shaped by people's sharing practices in the context of their wider social lives. Our analysis reveals the contribution that shared resources make to mobile conversations: they respond to and anticipate other contributions, acting as a focal point for online discussion as their meanings are co-constructed and negotiated by interlocutors. This ritual of sharing and appreciation represents a resourceful way in which people vie for others' attention, and display their own attentiveness, in mobile interactions, while allowing interactants to navigate between their online and offline engagements.

Mobile Conversations

This chapter starts from the assumption that exchanges conducted via mobile messaging can be analysed as a form of conversation (Giles et al. 2015, 2017; Paulus et al. 2016; Stommel et al. 2017). One key condition of mobile conversations is the lack of synchronicity, in the sense that message production and reception does not occur simultaneously, and recipients do not have access to a sender's message until it is fully formed and sent (Garcia and Jacobs 1999). As a result, the constraints that shape spoken face-to-face interaction do not apply; messages can be produced and sent at any time and there is no need for interactants to negotiate or compete for the 'conversational floor' (Meiler

2021). In other words, when it comes to mobile messaging, people do not need to engage in turn-taking in the same way as in spoken interaction, and nor do they have the means to do so (Beißwenger 2008). Rather than taking a turn, senders contribute to an unfolding interaction, potentially producing and sending messages at the same time as other interactants and responding to selected messages in an order that they deem appropriate. The fact that contributions to a mobile interaction are determined not by a turn-taking mechanism but by the timing of an individually produced message challenges the link between adjacency and conditional relevance. Rather than adjacency pairs, digital conversations are thus more accurately characterised by what König (2019) calls 'paired actions', in which a first part anticipates a second part which may be neither temporally nor spatially adjacent. In this chapter, we argue that this lack of synchronicity and adjacency makes possible an interactional space in which people share multimodal resources with which recipients can choose to engage or not.

Key to this argument is the way in which contributions to mobile conversations can incorporate various digital and networked resources available to smartphone users (Androutsopoulos 2014). Recent conversational analysis of embodied spoken exchanges points to the way in which social actions are accomplished through the involvement of entire bodies including body positioning, gestures, facial expressions and the handling of objects (Depperman and Streeck 2018), as well as sensory practices of gaze and touch (Mondada 2018). In digitally mediated interaction, users contend with a different set of resources. Much of the research on emoji and other *graphicons* (Herring and Dainas 2017) draws on survey and interview data or lab-based experiments (Tang and Hew 2019) to elicit participants' uses of and responses to them. Analysis of interactional data tends to focus on open social network sites and media-sharing platforms (Herring and Dainas 2017; Ge and Herring 2019; Herring et al. 2020), and somewhat less has been written about the use of multiple modes in closed synchronous interactions on interactive multimodal platforms like WhatsApp (though see Al Rashdi 2018; Panckhurst and Frontini 2020; Siever 2016; Siebenhaar 2016). Research across public and private online spaces has tended to take a quantitative approach resulting, for example, in lists of pragmatic functions fulfilled by graphicons (e.g., Herring and Dainas 2017). The tendency is to isolate particular graphicons and identify patterns in how they are being used, for example, the extent to which graphicons such as emoji can stand alone or are used to support or inflect verbal written language (e.g., Panckhurst and Frontini 2020). Such research has been useful in pinpointing the pragmatic functions of graphicons in use, but it does little to explain the complexities of individual users' wider communicative practices, running the risk of under- or overstating the role of isolated signs.

This chapter builds on this research in exploring how a range of different linguistic and multimodal signs are embedded in particular platforms and deployed in the course of unfolding exchanges. Our analysis of these often intimate conversations shows how multiple modes are brought together in closed groups and one-to-one chats in new ritualised practices to maintain and strengthen intimate relationships and get things done, while allowing individuals to contribute in ways appropriate to their individual circumstances.

Nested Linguistic and Multimodal Resources

As discussed in Chapter 4, internet and digital technologies have made available a wide range of potentially meaningful semiotic resources which were not typically accessible to most ordinary people in a pre-digital world (Williams 2009). The semiotic resources embedded into digital and mobile-enabled spaces can for present purposes be grouped into three categories:

1. Linguistic and multimodal signs brought along by users from their offline contexts and collaboratively reconstructed in mobile interactions.
2. Linguistic and multimodal signs made available through particular apps or platforms.
3. Linguistic and multimodal signs accessible through the wider network; e.g., by sharing links or copying and pasting from other sites.

The first category includes elements of different language-varieties, registers, styles, figurative devices and stance markers which have been explored in a range of studies focusing on, for example, regional variation and dialectal spelling (Hillewart 2015; Ilbury 2019; Jones 2016) and linguistic creativity (Tagg 2013; Littlemore and Tagg 2016), often highlighting the way in which offline contexts and identities are made relevant in online interactions. Also included in this category are photos and videos taken, usually by the user, of their own physical contexts in ways that not only provide a direct window onto their world, inviting the interlocutor in, but often index the user's perspective on – or interpretation of – a situation through gaze, proximity and choice of frame (Zhao and Zappavigna 2018). Jones (2020) argues that mobile photography goes beyond the representation of perspective to communicate 'the embodied experience of the visual'; that is, to involve others in the physical experience of being there. This can also be accomplished through the choice of other lexical or visual resources that act as a commentary on the external world (Lyons and Tagg 2021). We can thus see the sharing of such resources as acts of self-disclosure – directly revealing something of a person's immediate context to an otherwise physically distanced interlocutor – conferring on an interlocutor 'the right to look' (Jones 2020) and heightening social proximity and intimacy (Laurenceau et al. 1998). As Venema and Lobinger (2020) show, photos enable the representation and expression of self and the materialisation of memories and as such are key resources for maintaining close relationships.

Resources made available within the online space, the second category, include typeface, font, layout, background design and colour, each of which may be offered to users as a set of choices or be pre-configured. They also include keypad resources including punctuation and script (Androutsopoulos 2015) and in-built functionalities such as the ability to design one's own profile and to name groups, as well as sets of pre-configured graphicons such as emoji, stickers and GIFs. These graphicons fulfil a range of contextualised pragmatic functions (Panckhurst and Frontini 2020). Importantly, as with photos, graphicons have been seen to increase the sense of social connection and intimacy between users (Janssen et al. 2014), especially in the case of dynamic graphicons (Tung and Deng 2007) and detailed stickers resembling non-verbal cues in offline contexts (Wang 2016). Although different graphicon sets (such as emoticons and emoji) are sometimes conflated, there are differences in how they are perceived and used; for example, emoji may be seen as semantically richer than emoticons (Chen et al. 2017); and stickers – 'larger, more elaborate, character-driven illustrations or animations to which text is sometimes attached' (Konrad et al. 2020, p. 217) – are potentially perceived as more 'expressive' (Tang and Hew 2019, p. 2459) than emoji. Although stickers can be personalised by users (Tang and Hew 2019), these pre-configured resources are generally designed by software developers driven primarily by commercial interests (Djonov and van Leeuwen 2017) and as such must often be appropriated by users in creative and resourceful ways to fulfil their communicative needs. In this regard, the potential ambiguity of many of these in-built signs may be a strength (Pohl et al. 2017) which users can exploit in idiosyncratic ways, with playfulness adding to the impact of graphicons on increasing social connection (Hsieh and Tseng 2017) and – as demonstrated in our analysis – managing interactional expectations in light of user autonomy.

In contrast, networked resources (the final category) are not available within the app through which a user is interacting, but instead involve bringing in artefacts – tools or resources collectively imbued by cultural meaning – from elsewhere on the internet or 'the network' (Androutsopoulos 2015). What this effectively means is that users can embed globally circulating (commercial or grassroots) resources in their posts, often localising them for a new audience and appropriating them for individual ends. Bitmoji apps, for example, enable people to customise their own emoji and then insert them into interactions taking place on communication apps such as WhatsApp, Twitter or Snapchat. Networked resources can be copied, commented on or otherwise evaluated, or 'remixed' in creative, locally relevant ways. Examples include sampling and remixing (Williams 2009), video buffalaxing (Leppänen and Elo 2015) and memes (Luega 2020). Androutsopoulos (2010: 210) refers to these as 'vernacular spectacles' – typically low-budget but often very popular creations which sit 'at the core of a flourishing culture of media reproduction'. In this chapter, we show how networked and other resources are similarly put on display in closed mobile messaging groups for recipients' evaluation and appreciation through ritualised acts of sharing.

Sharing in Mobile Conversations

The concept of 'sharing' is associated with online practices on social media sites such as Facebook and Twitter. As John (2017) argues, the positive, open, collaborative connotations of the concept of sharing serve as a means for social media companies to sell products and encourage participation. In contrast to public online sharing on open social media sites, acts of sharing in closed spaces of mobile communication and between more intimate interlocutors can have different social meanings and fulfil different communicative functions. Social media audiences on sites like Facebook are typically both large and highly diverse, as well as unknown and invisible, in the sense that a user does not know who exactly among their audience will read and respond to their post (Tagg and Seargeant 2014). In the mobile messaging contexts discussed in this chapter, users interact either in a one-to-one situation or with a much smaller closed group and, thus, their posts are more narrowly targeted at a particular audience; presumably, they can also assume a more consistent level of background knowledge and shared communication history, and thus greater levels of trust and intimacy (Lyons 2020). In these contexts, sharing may be more interactionally oriented than on public media sites; that is, designed primarily to facilitate relationship maintenance – through, for example, provoking amusement or exploiting shared communicative histories.

From a sociolinguistics perspective, sharing can be seen as an interaction ritual, a repeated and conventionalised practice which accrues a particular significance for participants and affirms existing social structures (Goffman 1967). As a ritual, sharing involves the detaching of a text or artefact from its original context and its embedding in a new context – such as a WhatsApp group – an act which inevitably charges it with new social meaning. This means that sharing can be seen as an act of localisation or personalisation, whereby an artefact is appropriated, redesigned and reinterpreted for – and with shared knowledge of – a particular audience. Androutsopoulos (2014) suggests that such acts of entextualisation involve three main stages: the *selection* of semiotic resources; the *styling* of these resources for presentation in a new context; and *negotiation* with other users. How posts are selected (what is chosen for sharing), styled (how sharing is carried out) and negotiated (discussed with others) indexes users' orientations to each other and their perceptions of the audience's shared contextual frame: in Androutsopoulos's (2014: 6) words, '[u]nderstanding such moments and participating in their interactive negotiation is contingent on the background knowledge and the linguistic resources that members of the networked audience have in common with the sharer'. So sharing both presupposes, and works to reaffirm, existing affiliations between users. It also adds to the pool of in-group knowledge shared by an online group, shaping existing relationships within and beyond the immediate group.

Negotiation – the ways in which other users respond to the shared media, indirectly evaluating its selection and styling and thus performing varying degrees of (dis)alignment – is key to understanding sharing as an act of entextualisation. In relation to the posting of selfies and spoof videos, Georgakopoulou (2017: 182) shows how acts of sharing are likely met with expressions of ritual appreciation and knowing participation. *Ritual appreciation* refers to 'positive assessments of the post and/or poster, expressed in highly conventionalized language coupled with emoji', a practice which appears to describe Sally and Grace's responses in Figure 5.1. *Knowing participation* refers to users 'bringing in and displaying knowledge from offline, preposting activities or any other knowledge specific to the post or poster' – in other words, drawing on the existing shared communicative histories and backgrounds which may be indexed by the act of sharing. These acts of (dis) alignment serve to signal affiliation and potentially heighten intimacy.

These sharing rituals have parallels with those of digital gift giving. The rituals and principles of gift giving – chiefly the obligation to give, receive and reciprocate – underpin social cohesion and relationships across cultures (Mauss 2002) and shape the use of mobile media. Media practices both recreate existing traditions of exchange and reciprocity and extend them. For example, in 2015, WeChat developed an app that enabled Chinese people to send virtual 'red pockets' (envelopes of money) (Hjorth et al. 2020: 83). Less explicit, small daily 'check-ins' can also be seen as gift-giving, as can the sharing of everyday information and of one's location, while more recent work has focused on the sharing of photos and graphicons as digital gifts (Hjorth et al. 2020). Taylor and Harper (2003) note that teenagers felt obliged to respond and reciprocate in text message exchanges. In contrast, our analysis shows how our participants harness the affordances and conditions of mobile messaging to create a new form of ritualised sharing practice which disrupts the obligation to respond and reciprocate in the ways documented in previous studies.

Joe, Marta and Joanne: Polymedia Repertoires and Sharing

In the rest of this chapter, we explore the mobile resourcefulness of three of our participants, each of whom drew on a range of semiotic resources across different modes in their mobile communications: Joe, who moved to Birmingham from Hong Kong as a child; Marta, a Polish-born artist and actor based in London; and Joanne from mainland China, an adviser at the Chinese Community Centre in Birmingham. In interactions with those close to them, all three regularly embed multimodal resources into mobile messaging exchanges as part of their polymedia repertoires, exploiting these in the mobile messaging environment to remediate existing social relationships through emerging ritualised practices. Below we look in turn at selected exchanges carried out by each user, focusing on how they exploit affordances of the mobile phone and particular messaging apps, as well as drawing on their own multiple and shifting contexts.

Joe

Conversational Contributions to an Unfolding Interaction

Figure 5.2 presents an excerpt from a WhatsApp conversation between Joe and Sally, a close friend and manager of Joe's beauty salon. The conversation we are interested in starts 'Yesterday' (Monday 7th December 2015) at 19:45. It highlights the way in which acts of sharing are exploited to initiate or complete paired actions within an ongoing conversation.

Joe initiates the conversation with a contribution comprising a screenshot of an online discount voucher for a 'Live Escape Game for Two to Six People at Clue HQ Birmingham'. Although the screenshot is not accompanied by a written explanation, Joe's contribution is interpreted by his interlocutor apparently as it is intended – as an offer or a suggestion and therefore the first half of a paired action. The lack of verbal text which might *demand* a reply supports the reading of this as an offer, an interpretation which finds a parallel in Kress and van Leeuwen's (1996) distinction between 'demand' and 'offer' images, where the former is established through direct gaze with the viewer – inviting the viewer to examine and evaluate the content – while the latter engages the viewer only indirectly and impersonally. It is clear that Sally interprets it as a suggestion, as evident in her response, *Awww if pregnant women can do it I will soooooo go*, which can be categorised as an *acceptance* in a paired action of *offer* → *acceptance*. Her contribution (sent at 19:46), which is temporally and spatially adjacent, exhibits elements of ritual appreciation in the letter repetition or 'flooding' (*Awww*

Figure 5.2 Sharing a screenshot on WhatsApp.

and *soooooo*); but it also shows her knowing participation by raising the matter of her pregnancy as a relevant issue. The conversation continues ten minutes later (the delay likely occasioned by Joe's offline activities) with Joe offering a 'non-minimal third turn', in which he picks up on Sally's reference to her pregnancy and suggests she should call them 'to find out': his contribution is functionally dependent on Sally's previous contribution in that it completes a *problem* → *solution* pair. The coherence of this snippet of conversation is maintained throughout by anaphoric references back to 'doing' the game (*if pregnant women can do it, would be cool to do*). This reinforces the intended meaning of the act of sharing as an offer; putting something forward that they could do, if it engaged Sally's interest.

Using and sharing discount offers is a regular practice for this friend network, and in this way the meaning of any one instance is shaped by the wider practices and media environments in which these resources are embedded. For example, Joe shares a Groupon voucher for the pub Fiddle and Bone in response to his friend Laura's query 'Where is it?' when he tries to persuade her to join him for dinner (*More from Less*, Wednesday 11th November). This regular practice does not require any explanatory text to accompany the discount vouchers and nor does it invite discussion of its intended meaning; instead, each act of sharing reinforces the group's practice and triggers the expected responses. In interview, Joe pointed to their long history on WhatsApp – his app records that members of one group, *Eating N Drinking*, had sent 1,200 media resources (not all of which we collected) – commenting:

Joe: sometimes you put something on, you already know exactly what it's about, anything to do with Greggs [a chain bakery in the UK] is to do with Sally, because she loves Greggs, so anything like that we know it's a joke about her

Joe and Sally's conversation about the discount continued, as shown in Figure 5.3. At 19:57, Joe sends two messages in quick succession: one which

Figure 5.3 Inviting someone into the moment through WhatsApp.

we have already discussed as completing a *problem → solution* paired action (*Maybe call to find out*), and a second which initiates a new pair: *How's ur beef stew?*. This 'chunking' of Joe's message into two transmissions appears to mark the change in topic, which then in turn marks the start of a new pair.

The reference to Sally's beef stew highlights their shared communicative history, which encompasses Joe's knowledge of what Sally was having for dinner and their shared interest in food (as we shall see later, both Sally and Joe also belong to the WhatsApp group *Eating N Drinking*). Sally replies around 15 minutes later, expressing her approval of the stew through emotive vocabulary and a heart-eyed emoji, and then asks Joe *what you got?*, an informal colloquial phrasing or brought-along resource which may add to the intimacy of the exchange. Joe responds immediately, not with a verbal answer but with a photo of his half-eaten meal: he completes the *question → answer* paired action through a process of entextualisation, by which the immediate action of eating is captured and recontextualised within the digital conversation, becoming an object which can be negotiated and revised (Jones 2010). The act of entextualisation does not serve primarily to address Sally's question but rather to invite her into the moment, the half-eaten food and the cutlery resting on his plate conveying the embodied experience – the taste and texture – of the meal (Jones 2020). Key to its impact is the way in which the photo – as an implied selfie which suggests but does not depict the photo-taker themselves (Zhao and Zappavigna 2018) – invites Sally to experience the scene from Joe's perspective. Interestingly, although a second plate is visible in the photo, Joe's dining partner is excluded from the photo in a way that adds to the intimacy being constructed between Joe and Sally in the intersection of the offline (the sensory experience of the meal) and the online. The text accompanying the photo, *Groupon*, adds a wry evaluation which further heightens the intimacy through its reference to the established group practice. The brevity of the explanation suggests knowing participation through their familiarity both with Groupon and the group's frequent use of it. Again, Sally's subsequent contribution shows elements of ritual appreciation, this time with emoji flooding, a common response to shared pictures of food across this dataset and others (Tagg and Seargeant 2012). The sharing or offering of the picture not only completes the *question → answer* pair but also instigates a subsequent paired action which we describe as *share → show appreciation*, which involves an act of sharing typically followed by ritual appreciation and/or knowing participation. As we shall see, *share → show appreciation* is a popular practice across our datasets.

The resourcefulness evident in this exchange lies in the way in which the functionalities of the mobile phone and the mobile messaging app – namely, the ability both to take photos and to embed them within interactions – are collaboratively taken up by participants both to facilitate their virtual conversation and to open it up to other virtual and physical contexts beyond the immediate communicative space. The harnessing of these affordances for interpersonal functions prompts the eventual emergence of new conventional or ritualised practices, as evidenced by the paired action *share → show appreciation*, which in turn shape the kinds of relationship it is possible to have. This is further evidenced by data from Joe's group chats below.

Sharing as a Focus for Attention

In more focused instances of sharing, resources are offered to others for comment and engagement. In these moments, resources are carefully selected and styled for a particular group of interlocutors, before being further recontextualised through group negotiation and discussion often in ways not apparently intended by the sender.

The extract in Figure 5.4 a, b, c is taken from the WhatsApp group *Eating N Drinking*, which includes Joe and his partner Drew and two of his closest

Figure 5.4a Creating a focus for attention in a WhatsApp group (cont.)

Figure 5.4b Creating a focus for attention in a WhatsApp group (cont.)

friends: Sally and Grace. As the group name suggests, one of their interests is eating out. In this case, however, Grace shares a photo of her son Finn's injury (Friday 8th January at 20:46).

The extract shows how Grace takes the floor in order to carry out an extended act of sharing which seems to be triggered by her having just responded to Joe's previous message (*Ooooo let me check X*); not only is she prompted to share her news because she has her phone in her hand but because this channel of communication (the WhatsApp group) has been 'renewed' by Joe, a term Spilioti (2011: 81) uses in discussing channels that are 'perpetually open' but momentarily suspended through lack of immediate use. Grace's subsequent turns are marked off from the surrounding discourse by her opening utterance *Look what happened to our Finn!* and held up for evaluation and comment (Maybin and Swann 2007). Her contribution brings together multiple modal resources, including verbal text, image and emoji.

Grace introduces the shared photo with two verbal explanations, the first of which sets up the photo as the main communicative event (*Look what*

Figure 5.4c Creating a focus for attention in a WhatsApp group.

happened to our Finn!), outlines the background to the photo, and uses emoji to frame the way in which the photo should be interpreted. In this case, the shocked face emoji presumably indicates her initial response to the incident – what Herring and Dainas (2017) call 'reaction': an emotion in response to something posted – while the grinning face is an instance of tone modification which works to reassure her friends. This second stance is reflected in her use of colloquial respellings *playin* ('playing') and *an* ('and') which suggest casual informality (although this is also a style adopted by Grace throughout her messages so may have no marked meaning here). Grace's second verbal explanation is sent after the photo and appears to direct her friends' specific attention to what is important about the photo. Her friends' responses suggest that it is the photo, rather than the written explanations, which generates further conversation and social alignment most effectively.

The photo elicits both ritual appreciation – as in Sally's *Omfg* and emoji flooding – and further conversation, as Sally asks for details. Sally's query

(*Was it a fight?*) appears not to have fully taken into account Grace's verbal explanation that Finn 'was playin about' and 'banged his face', but seems rather to be responding primarily to the shared photo. This prompts Grace to repeat her explanation, again with colloquial respellings and emoji; she also uses question marks expressively to indicate her doubt about her son's unlikely sounding story (*his friend was tryin to pick him up??*).

There is then a pause before Drew responds 20 minutes later. Drew's contributions include a range of involvement strategies, designed to show alignment and affiliation with Grace and the group (Tannen 1989). Firstly, he uses both ritual appreciation (*Omg*) and playful alliterative remarks about Finn's 'bad boy bruise' and his 'swish smile', as well as knowing participation when he alludes to Finn's character (*gay Finnie*) and to those of Grace and her partner Mike. Secondly, and most interestingly perhaps, Drew re-interprets the photo, recontextualising Finn not as a victim with a black eye, but as a smug and self-satisfied fighter. Drew explains his position by picking up on a detail in the photo, the nature of Finn's smile. According to Tannen (1989), 'attention to detail is a sign of intimacy' (p. 162) which serves to convey 'a metamessage of rapport, of caring' (p. 149) because it indicates interest: here, it suggests that Drew is paying attention. Tannen refers to this as displaying listenership, which corresponds to Drew's careful *looking* in this case. Furthermore, Drew's reinterpretation is provocative and the fact that he feels he can (and does) get away with it further indexes a close relationship. As Carter (2007: 165) notes in his study of language creativity, playfulness is more likely to take place between intimates where relations are close and socially symmetrical, in part because of the risk involved in pushing at accepted boundaries. Drew's playful reinterpretation is indeed accepted in a follow-up turn from Grace: the emoji at the start of her turn serve as expressive response markers to indicate her appreciation, before she confirms that Finn is feeling very pleased with himself.

In these ritualised exchanges, shared photos are put on display before a group of friends who are invited to respond. Both Sally and Drew take their own stance towards the photo, rather than being driven by the verbal content of Grace's surrounding comments. Their take is interactively validated by the group, indicating acceptance of interactional autonomy. Their responses are resourceful in the way they involve the collaborative harnessing of semiotic resources made available by the mobile phone to index attention and attentiveness. This resourcefulness is thus associated with bolstering social involvement and alignment between autonomous agents. A response is not required from each interactant and, on this occasion, Joe does not contribute. WhatsApp's asynchronous nature, affirmed through repeated practice, and facilitated by the playful framing of the interaction, mitigates the potential face threat posed by not receiving a response, making reciprocity not strictly required.

Joe told us in interview that sharing within his networks is driven primarily by a desire to maintain close social relationships through amusement, enjoyment, or what Joe in interview called 'fun':

Joe: I think it's just for fun ... it's just for fun, pictures of me, of camping, videos ... it's just for sharing things with friends, I think ... because these two are my best friends, Grace and Sally, so anything funny we just share

Overall, the group's acts of mobile resourcefulness point to the ways in which people start to extend or alter their practices in ways that are shaped by the situated uses of technology. The harnessing of multimodal resources within the context of a group chat for the purposes of interpersonal alignment creates a new kind of space for enacting friendship, one which relies less on synchronous exchange but rather on a more distributed or 'ambient' (Zappavigna 2012) online social presence. People in this communicative space – which runs parallel, and interweaves with, multiple other virtual and physical contexts – share resources in order to draw their friends' attention, and showing attentiveness becomes a key marker of friendship. We return to these themes in discussion of Marta's exchanges below.

Marta

Location Sharing

Marta and her London-based Polish friends used WhatsApp frequently to micro-coordinate the day's events and establish exact locations for meetings and get-togethers, a typical function of mobile messaging (Ling and Yttri 2002). Few if any studies have discussed the role of sending one's 'current location' (on a map) in micro-coordination (although see Lyons and Ounoughi 2020). In Figure 5.5, Marta initiates communication with Marcel with her location on a map and then sends two other short messages *Laws?* and *Coffee?*, the two modes combining in complementary ways to complete the contribution.

It is likely that *Laws* is an autocorrect of the Polish word *kawa* ('coffee') which, as suggested by the speed of her third contribution, Marta then corrected. The use of an English word at this point illustrates how multilingual mobile phone users can draw on resources across their linguistic repertoires to overcome limitations of the technology – it is easier for Marta to type the English word than switch to the Polish keyboard setting, and she knows her

Figure 5.5 Sharing location on WhatsApp.

Figure 5.6 Location sharing as a conversational turn.

interlocutor will understand. In this case, neither Marta nor Marcel comment on either the initial mistake or the correction.

In a second example of location sharing in Figure 5.6, although Marcel sends only his location with no verbal explanation, his contribution elicits a clear and immediate response (*Pochlastam sie*, 'I'll slit my wrists') which seems to suggest that Marta is familiar with the place and which we interpret as exhibiting jealousy probably because she cannot – for whatever reason – be there (she goes on to write *Baw sie pysznie*, 'Have a great time', the emoticon :) indexing her shift in footing). This suggests that location being sent in such a way is received and processed as part of a conversation; it does not have to be specifically introduced or explained but is treated as equally valid to stating one's location verbally.

In sharing their location in this way, the friends resourcefully exploit the affordances of the mobile phone to create a locus of attention which invites – without demanding – contributions from those who are not physically present, and whose concurrent engagements are unknown to the sender. The practice is shaped not only by the interlocutors' interpersonal needs – their use of mobile messaging to set up meetings and exchange personal messages – but also by the casual and intimate nature of their existing relationship and their shared communicative history. It is a practice that is by its nature embedded in people's offline lives and physical activities and one which in turn potentially shapes their offline experiences, not only facilitating offline meetings but also bringing to the physical location participation and evaluation from virtual others.

Messaging on the Move

We now look in more depth at one snippet of Marta's WhatsApp interactions, this time taken from a group chat with Marcel and a friend of theirs, Klara. This exchange (starting in Figure 5.7) illustrates how attention is managed on WhatsApp through the harnessing of a range of available resources during the course of two of the participants' journey across London on the underground to the home of the third. The offline journey is indexed throughout

Updacie	M: Updacie [=Updacik, 'a little update']
Update	M: Update
Bede za godzinę jednak	M: I'll be there in an hour after all
Sorry pojebało mi sie	M: Sorry I fucked up
Jestem na East Acton i cisne dalej centralka na northolt	M: I'm at East Acton and I'm pushing onwards on the Central [line] towards Northolt
Za 5 stacji	M: In 5 stations
Super	K: Super

Figure 5.7 Sending updates via WhatsApp while on the move.

the conversation, with the travelling interlocutors calling in with updates on their progress as they micro-coordinate their arrival. *Updacie* – a non-word which results from Marta's attempt to write *updacik* (the English word *update* + Polish suffix, meaning 'little update') and which she corrects to *Update* – indexes the group's shared affiliation as London-based Poles. This initial message – and its intended reference to their common background – also acts as an alert or a summons, intended to attract the attention of Marcel and Klara, who are respectively travelling and busy preparing for the others' arrival. Marta then proceeds to update her friends on her progress.

Klara's role in the conversation appears to be that of central hub and also of providing motivation and encouragement (e.g., *Super*, a word of English origin now widely used by Polish speakers). Their distinct participant roles – Marta and Marcel moving through unfamiliar parts of London while Klara waits in her home – appear to shape the kind of posts they style and share. For her part, Klara draws her friends' attention to her immediate context – and their target destination – by taking and sending a photo of the food she has prepared and which is now ready on her table. On the one hand, taking and sending a photo is easier and quicker than describing the scene. On the other hand, Klara's photo provides a more direct representation of the food than a verbal description likely would and simultaneously invites the travellers into the transient moment and the physical space of her room (Jones 2020). The caption *Tu juz żarcie czeka...* (Here the grub is already waiting...') highlights the apparent function of the photo – a source of motivation, pointing to the travellers' end goal – with the ellipsis pointing to the anticipation of the party ahead. So, the focus is perhaps not on sharing her immediate embodied experience but on anticipating and making visible her interlocutors' soon-to-be experience.

As evident in Figures 5.8 and 5.9, the act of entextualisation holds up the food – and therefore Klara's selection and styling of the shared resource – as an object of evaluation. Her two interlocutors display their attentiveness – and their focus on their destination – with ritual appreciation realised through exclamations marked by punctuation and capitals, completing the paired action which we describe as *share* → *show appreciation*. The two responses parallel each other, one in Polish, one in English. We interpret Marcel's follow-up message (*!*) as completing his earlier turn, thus emphasising the parallel between the two ritualised responses, rather than responding to Marta's subsequent question about water.

In Figure 5.9, the two travellers continue to exchange messages in multiple interweaving conversational threads, drawing on various linguistic resources to manage the conversation and the other's attention. Klara then interrupts them with a post designed to grab their attention: a close up of a pack of water bottles with the stark verbal comment, *Starczy?* ('Enough?').

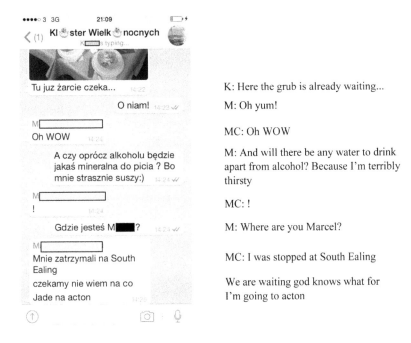

Figure 5.8 Expressing ritual appreciation through WhatsApp.

We might see this as the closure of *question → answer* paired action opened up by Marta's question about the water, in which the different elements or modes combine to create meaning: the caption 'Enough?' is an ironic statement, given the amount of water in the photo. A verbal description may have worked here – 'I have 30 bottles of water. Enough?' – but the photo serves to vividly and indisputably evidence the quantity in a way that a verbal statement would not, in an interesting (and perhaps intentional) parallel with the earlier food photo. The fact that the bottles are still wrapped is a visual clue which suggests she has bought these specially and is prepared for their visit. As with other exchanges between Marta and her friends, the selection and styling of this modal resource both plays a communicative function in the ongoing exchange – responding to Marta's question about water – and bolsters their already close relationships through playfulness and disclosure, while at the same time allowing the recipients to evaluate the availability of water for themselves.

This instance of mobile messaging on the move illustrates the complex ways in which WhatsApp, and the resources which the app makes

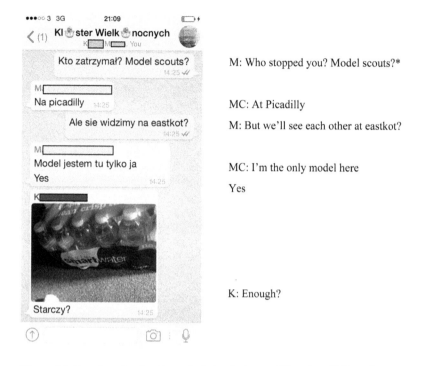

Figure 5.9 Drawing attention through photo sharing on WhatsApp. [*The reference here is unclear to us and is probably an in-group reference to an earlier, online or offline, exchange.]

available, have been taken up for the purposes of keeping in touch while in transit. The pursuit of these purposes is not new and cannot be seen as disrupting existing practice, but instead builds on practices of location-checking and micro-coordination made possible since the late 1990s by SMS text messaging (Ling and Yttri 2002; Tagg 2012). In the exchange explored here, the friends seek to similarly micro-coordinate their journeys, but in doing so draw on new affordances – photo-taking, group chats – that in turn enable them to extend and enrich the practice, creating a space in which multiple interlocutors can share and access updates and giving those travelling an insight into their destination before arrival. This space in turn pushes interlocutors to consider the ways in which attention can be managed in busy, fast-moving conditions. In effect, messaging on the move opens up the space available for interpersonal exchange – from an event itself to the preparatory and travel time before and after it – thus bolstering friendship ties.

Joanne

Joanne and her Hong Kong-born husband Vincent draw on the affordances of WeChat messaging to maintain and enhance their intimate relationship both through creating an ongoing channel of communication – one which extends into their working lives throughout the day – and through drawing playfully and knowingly on a set of shared multimodal and multilingual semiotic resources partly afforded by the messaging function of the app. In Figure 5.10, for example, Joanne's routine check-in ('what have you got for lunch') prompts the two to draw on written Chinese and English in naming various food items (*bread, coffee, yoghurt, satsuma, apple*).

Vincent appears to be deliberately and playfully echoing Joanne's use of *coffee* when he uses the English word *yoghurt*, thus showing his attentiveness to her language choices through parallelism (Tannen 1989) and pointing to the shared elements of their repertoires. Vincent also uses stickers and emoji, inserting two pre-configured images of Chinese characters and a picture of a banana rather than using verbal text. The use of an image at this point appears to parallel the use of English to name food items in their earlier contributions, marking the food items as distinct through a shift in mode. As with Edyta and her friend in Chapter 4, it is likely that Vincent is focused less on the content of their exchange and rather on humouring

J: <what have you got for lunch>

V: <just bread>

J: <and > coffee?

V: <yep but no>yogurt

J: <have some fruit>

V: <one piece of> banana

J: Satsuma. Apple

V: later

[J shares an article entitled as: Take a second thought before you eat bread]

Figure 5.10 Checking-in multimodally on WeChat.

his wife through attention to her semiotic choices. In the last contribution in Figure 5.10, sent the following day, Joanne makes her point not through her own words, but by posting an article entitled 'Take a second thought before you eat bread'. Sharing news stories is a frequent practice across Joanne's messages, as is discussion around health, and she exploits them resourcefully throughout her WeChat exchanges to signal her views about healthy food and to alert her friends and family (Lyons et al. 2019). In this case, Joanne's act of sharing serves to exploit the article's external authority in supporting her earlier suggestion that Vincent should not eat bread alone.

Throughout their conversations, they use both the simplified (Joanne) and traditional (Vincent) Chinese scripts, which could be interpreted as indexing their respective national identities, despite their common geographical location in the UK and their shared domestic context: Joanne is from mainland China, where the simplified script is used, while Vincent is from Hong Kong, which retains the traditional or complicated script. We observed a similar practice in WeChat messages between Kang Chen, the UK butcher from mainland China – who wrote in the simplified Chinese script – and the Hong Kong-origin restaurant owners in Birmingham who used the traditional script (see Chapter 3). As with the meat orders between the Mandarin-speaking butcher and the Cantonese-speaking restaurant owner, it is likely that Joanne and her husband have their chosen script set as default on their phones and so the choice may not be actively involved in interpersonal meaning-making.

The following example (Figure 5.11) is also illustrative of the way in which the pair draw on overlapping polymedia repertoires to establish intimacy in the communicative space of this mobile phone app. Joanne has just joked that she is so busy at work that she has not had time to go to the toilet.

Vincent's response to his wife's joke shows resourcefulness in its contextually relevant reinterpretation of a networked resource, namely a Chinese sticker showing a young Chinese man being stopped by a traffic policeman who gives him a fine and points against his licence. Stickers are currently more popular and more widely used in Asia than in Europe and used extensively in Chinese social media including WeChat (e.g., Konrad et al. 2020). Larger and more elaborate than emoji, stickers may be perceived by users as more expressive, especially when they evoke offline contexts (Wang 2016). In this case, the sticker again constitutes a conversational action which responds to Joanne's announcement and requires no introduction or commentary. In contrast to a verbal response, the sticker gives voice to Vincent's opinion of his wife's stated action but does so indirectly, through analogy with the communicative situation depicted in the sticker. As such, it exploits the potential ambiguity of graphicons for its effectiveness in this context; in the words of Pohl et al. (2017: 2), the 'meaning is fluid and subject to contextual and

J: really did wet my pants [smiley face]

V: [sends a photo bearing text saying <200 Yuan fine, plus 6 penalty points>]

J shares an article titled: <How many retired Chinese officials are staying in Canada? The Canadian police turned dumb at the truth!>

Figure 5.11 Sharing a sticker on WeChat.

cultural … interpretation'. The sticker both indexes and heightens a sense of intimacy between the couple, not least because of the layers of shared background knowledge that it assumes. On one level, the sticker assumes a shared understanding regarding the practice of sticker-use as part of their shared interactional history. On another level, the sticker assumes a shared cultural understanding in that it represents a typical scenario in mainland China where the traffic police play a prominent role in regulating drivers. The sticker here is also playful, the humour emerging partly because of the clash between contexts – the idea that you might be fined because you could not get to the toilet in time – which can be seen to increase intimacy and a sense of couplehood.

Interestingly, however, we found that Joanne's acts of sharing often went unacknowledged by her husband and other participants (see Figure 5.12). As mentioned above, she regularly shared WeChat articles, often on the subject of health and food. This practice can itself be seen as resourceful – an attempt to exploit the affordances of the app which was grounded in her existing interest in the subject and her desire to positively influence her social networks.

In seeking to explain this, we can point to our arguments regarding the ambient nature of multimodal sharing which does not always require the recipient to respond. In sharing these articles, without verbally directing her

J shares an article entitled as: <'how many retired Chinese officials are staying in Canada? The Canadian police turned dumb at the truth!.>

J shares an article entitled as: <only three photos but are worth millions>

J shares an article entitled as:< the top ten restaurants in Shenyang which I will definitely go no matter what.>

Figure 5.12 Sharing WeChat news articles.

interlocutors' attention to them or demanding a reply, Joanne achieves her purpose of informing or educating them without imposing on them the obligation to respond in particular ways. Her resourcefulness also recognises the potential inappropriateness of requiring recipients in this context to read long or complex articles, and instead grants them the autonomy to respond as they see fit. We have not had an opportunity to ask how Joanne felt about this or whether her interlocutors responded in other ways, by phoning her or talking about the articles in person. However, nowhere in the data have we found any indication that Joanne's sharing and the resulting interactional dynamics constituted an unaccepted practice in her network.

Conclusion

This chapter explored the ways in which interpersonal relationships are maintained and bolstered through sharing multimodal resources in closed mobile messaging groups and intimate one-to-one interactions. Our participants used mobile messaging to send photos which bridge both physical and social distance, allowing direct access to their 'real-world' settings and events and triggering displays of attentiveness and engagement, which demonstrate an appreciation of interlocutors' agency and autonomy. More focused acts of sharing are marked off from the general flow of the conversation and held up for social evaluation and for further acts of reinterpretation. As well as showing how people draw on the full range of resources made available to them in these spaces – not only those they bring along and collaboratively recontextualise, but also in-built app resources and globally circulating cultural artefacts – analysis of their sharing practices detailed how resources were *selected* and *styled* according to their perceived relevance to the audience. The ways in which acts of sharing were *negotiated* in the mobile conversations often showed both ritual appreciation (fairly formulaic and highly positive assessments) and knowing participation. However, in other cases, the sharing of resources became a focal point for discussion and competing interpretations.

The chapter suggests that multimodal sharing in mobile messaging contexts can be understood in terms of mobile resourcefulness; that is, as attempts to take advantage of complex nests of polymedia resources for interpersonal ends such as upholding friendships and engaging in social interactions. One way in which mobile resourcefulness manifests in interlocutors' exploitation of multimodal resources is in managing *attention*. By sharing a resource, senders provide a focus for shared attention, with which recipients can choose to engage, depending on such factors as their whereabouts, their availability and their parallel activities. Our data shows how sharing allows people to attract the attention of busy interlocutors who are simultaneously managing multiple threads of online conversation amidst offline activities. Shared content, in turn, draws attention to other spaces and activities, sometimes bringing the poster's immediate physical context into the mobile space and inviting responses. However, mobile conversations are not only about *getting* attention through sharing resources, but also selectively *paying* attention to what is being shared. The displays of ritual appreciation and knowing participation that follow acts of sharing point to the importance of displaying one's attentiveness. As such, mobile conversations are managed cognitively and socially through attention structures (Jones 2010). An analogy can be made with spoken conversation in which participants show they are listening through adopting involvement strategies and performing 'listenership'. However, showing attentiveness takes on a particular significance in online interactions, given that online presence in textual contexts can *only* be indicated through users' contributions (with the exception perhaps of the blue tick in WhatsApp which indicates that a message has been read). As such, sharing, ritual appreciation and knowing participation may be seen as (new) involvement strategies designed to cope with familiar interactional demands shaped by the nature and constraints of mobile conversations (cf. Herring 1999). Such mobile resourcefulness is mundane and yet fundamental to the remediation of friendships through mobile communication in contemporary society.

6 Conclusion

In this concluding chapter, we reflect on what the book has achieved and point to the potential of mobile resourcefulness for explaining how people negotiate contemporary polymedia repertoires, and in so doing potentially resist the dominant narratives of technology companies. We started this book by asking what it means to be part of a society in which much of our communication is mediated by technology: how do technologies such as mobile messaging apps fit into and shape people's lives, and how do people appropriate the technology to carry out everyday tasks, express themselves and maintain social relationships? By focusing on people's resourcefulness in harnessing digital and mobile media to their own ends, this book unpicked the role that technologies play in the contemporary everyday, shaping but also shaped by people's communicative practices and their wider social and economic lives. Our post-digital approach – whereby digitally mediated communication is explored as part of individuals' communicative repertoires from the perspective of a largely 'offline' ethnography – paves the way for future research, and in what follows we suggest how the approach could be further developed to better understand contemporary communication.

Mobile Resourcefulness, Polymedia Repertoires and Attention

The concept of mobile resourcefulness emerged from our observations of the ways in which our participants adopted new technologies and technologically enabled practices, and collaboratively adapted them to pursue their existing communicative goals and identity projects. We noted that it was only over time that these new technology uses led our participants to extend or alter their existing practices, a process that was influenced in part by their commercial activities and in part by their relational needs. We also found that mobile resourcefulness was shaped by our participants' polymedia

DOI: 10.4324/9780429031465-6

repertoires, just as their repertoires were shaped by their resourcefulness. Edyta, for example, started using her mobile phone to fill the gap left in her polymedia repertoire by her landline, thereby remediating her business practices with suppliers and customers and creating the opportunity for new ways of getting things done and new kinds of relationships. This resourcefulness also resulted, among other things, in the social meaning of different apps being shaped by their very different uses, with, for example, Viber used by Edyta with intimates and SMS text messaging with suppliers.

Mobile resourcefulness manifested in distinct ways across our participants' practices. As discussed in Chapter 3, Joanne and her friend's decision to exploit the 'WeChat Store' to set up their e-business was grounded in their wider sociotechnical context, driven not only by the popularity of WeChat Store and by economic imperative but by their understanding of their own geographic locations and social networks – the fact that Joanne was in the UK and could source products which could then be sold by Zhao in China. They also drew on their familiarity with other functionalities of WeChat, such as the messaging and voice functions – which they used to plan and carry out their business at a distance – and their phone cameras to take and share photos of products. For Kang Chen, his links with China initially enabled the emergence of new working practices. He was encouraged to download the app by his brother (via his wife), who wished to stay in touch with him from China. Kang Chen and local Chinese restaurant owners then quickly recognised the potential WeChat offered for making meat-ordering more convenient and efficient, particularly in the busy contexts in which they worked and the hectic pace of their everyday lives. This in turn began to alter how the practice was carried out, creating a permanent record of transactions and a new business-related register. Resourceful in his adoption of the affordances of the app, by the time we met him, Kang Chen claimed not to be able to run his business without it. Similarly, as we saw in Chapter 4, Edyta's use of her mobile phone for commercial purposes was grounded in the wider socio-economic environment of their family business. Initially adopted when Edyta's landline stopped working, she and her interlocutors – both suppliers and customers – exploited mobile messaging to carry out practices which had once been fulfilled by other means, such as face-to-face visits or landline calls, and which were shaped by existing relationships and linguistic registers. In turn, the use of mobile messaging extended what was possible in ways that were experienced both as beneficial – in that customers could enact pre-order routines and thus avoid a wasted trip to the shop – and as unwelcome, such as the tendency for the practice to blur the boundaries between Edyta's working and home life.

In contrast to the commercial practices above, Winnie's resourcefulness lay in the way she embedded the new mobile technologies into her enactment of diverse social roles, and drew on them to maintain and extend her personal values. Her technology uptake was supported by both family and friends, with her son giving her his old phone and setting up their family WhatsApp group, and her friend scaffolding her acquisition of features of what has been described elsewhere as 'txtspk'. Her online writing practices were shaped by existing writing conventions and values such as politeness and language correctness, and grounded in attempts to maintain intimate and social relationships. In mobile interactions, Winnie was exposed to new forms of written expression and prompted by her love of learning to understand these new conventions (e.g., unfamiliar abbreviations) and incorporate them into her own repertoire. This expanding repertoire in turn enabled Winnie to both consolidate and extend her social relations, and in particular to establish her emerging relationship with her new daughter-in-law. As such, Winnie's use of WhatsApp and other mobile phone features was grounded in her own identity project and social milieu, and it was only gradually that she drew on the affordances to alter her practices and social relations.

These case studies illustrate some of the ways in which mobile resourcefulness is realised in everyday practice. Taken together, they show that, far from being passive technology users, our participants actively harness the technologies available to them for their own purposes in ways which are not always intended by media companies.

The case studies also draw attention to the ways in which mobile resourcefulness is realised in interaction. Chapter 3 made clear that mobile resourcefulness is not something that an individual brings *a priori* to a social encounter; instead, what is often perceived as individual agency is distributed across the multiple people, artefacts, technologies, discourses and contexts that contribute to a social action. Detailed attention to the minutiae of our participants' mobile exchanges enabled us to explore the role of interaction in facilitating and shaping mobile resourcefulness. Many of the practices and associated linguistic registers outlined above emerged through interaction, as interlocutors negotiated overlapping repertoires in order to carry out shared communicative activities. For example, we saw how Edyta and her suppliers discursively co-constructed an informal business register through which supplies could be efficiently negotiated; this register oriented to the norms of Polish-language transactions and of the UK context in which they were conducted, as well as the interactants' ongoing relationships. In Chapter 5, we explored how multimedia resources were shared and collaboratively taken up in order to facilitate conversation and provide insights into each other's physical contexts, while recognising the other demands on interactants' attention. It was this interaction which prompted the emergence of a conventional practice of *share → show appreciation*, and which in turn created new spaces for the enactment of friendship. In Marta's case, mobile messaging opened up a space in which a group of friends could share updates from their respective locations while on the move, inviting others into their immediate physical space and extending the opportunity for social contact beyond their eventual offline get-together. In Joe's case, the emergent space was similarly one characterised by a kind of ambient affiliation, in which friends were brought together around shared multi-modal resources and where the temporal alignment of posts and responses was less important than the freedom to choose when and whether to contribute by displaying attentiveness. For Joanne, the interactional dynamic of WeChat afforded the sharing of her views on healthy eating in a way that respected her contacts' autonomy as individuals juggling the many demands on their time. As with Marta and Joe, new interactional dynamics emerged through habitual shared practice, shaped by people's perceptions of what a digital context affords.

In a methodological aside, the likelihood that Joanne and her interactants discussed her WeChat articles elsewhere – and that their selection may have been triggered in the first place in interactional contexts outside the app – points to the need for post-digital ethnography in understanding the flow of relationships and interactions across media. In this case, we were not able to discuss this further with Joanne and ideally this would need to be possible in research seeking to understand mobile resourcefulness. The inter-active nature of mobile resourcefulness also requires an approach which explores individuals' and groups' mobile communication over time, tracing and explaining the emergence of shared practices such as the sharing of WeChat articles, discount vouchers or stickers. We showed the potential of a diachronic approach by documenting the process by which Joanne and Zhao set up their e-business, the emergence of the virtual noticeboard at the Birmingham butcher stall, and the factors that lay behind Edyta remediating her business practices through her mobile. This long-term perspective is crucial in understanding how practices are remediated and refashioned through new technologies.

A final factor is the importance of *attention* for understanding resource-fulness in relation to polymedia repertoires. Much has been written about the contemporary attention economy in reference to the ways in which corporations, public figures and political organisations work to capitalise on the attention of their consumers and publics, through such attention-grabbing strategies as sensationalised language, notifications and person-alisation algorithms that purportedly provide users with what they want to see (Jones and Hafner 2021). Such accounts position users as relatively passive in their exploitation by advertising and social media companies, or at least relatively powerless to resist. But, as we have seen, the management of attention is also increasingly key to understanding how ordinary people navigate personal and social mediascapes and polymedia resources (Jones 2010). In Chapter 5, we looked at the ways in which users of mobile messaging display various linguistic and multimodal signs in a way which creates a focus for attention, acknowledging recipients' autonomy while providing an opportunity for friendship to be enacted through displays of attentiveness. Attention is also a key factor in people's negotiation of their polymedia repertoires at other levels of expression, shaped by media ideologies which determine how people evaluate the appropriate uses of different devices, platforms and apps. Crucial questions around attention include how and why people attend to their mobile phones and other devices in the midst of multiple physical activities in shifting offline contexts, and how interlocutors perceive and respond to this. As we saw in the book, meat-ordering through WeChat allows Kang Chen to conduct his offline work at the stall without unwelcome interruptions. Joe similarly told us in interview that he would not answer messages or voice calls while attending to customers at work (and, indeed, many of the mobile messaging exchanges we collected from Joe took place after work). In contrast, Edyta's customers gain her attention through their access to her mobile phone and resourceful use of humour and visual signs. Edyta feels obliged to respond to their messages but resents their intrusion into other aspects of her life. Each of these can be seen as an attempt to gain, keep, manage and display attention, manifested in everyday practices, making attention key to understanding how polymedia repertoires are resourcefully deployed in contemporary social interaction. All of this calls for the development of approaches which chart the intersecting rhythms of online and offline encounters throughout the course of individuals' daily interactions.

The Scope of Mobile Resourcefulness

Mobile resourcefulness contributes to our understanding of how mobile communication technologies are being used by individuals and the implications of this use for people's social lives and relations. On the one hand, the concept elaborates on the situated nature of technology use by providing a framework for understanding the process by which users adopt a new technology to carry out existing communicative practices. This includes understanding how these practices – along with people's perceived needs – then shift in line with their perception of the affordances of the new technology. Such a process focuses attention on continuity in practice and the remediation of existing practices through new technologies, rather than assuming behaviour is determined by particular technologies. On the other hand, mobile resourcefulness draws attention to the distributed nature of agency, and to the way in which an apparent decision at any one time emerges as the result of complex intersections between people, places, objects and discourses. This extends its relevance beyond foregrounding the role of people's agency in shaping their technology use, and in particular their ability to collaboratively harness technological affordances to fulfil joint communicative goals. As such, resourcefulness explains how and why technologies get taken up in particular ways, driven and shaped by a confluence of situational factors.

Our intention is not to use mobile resourcefulness to suggest that some people are more resourceful than others, and that some technology uses reflect resourcefulness in ways that others do not. Instead, we see resourcefulness as a *lens* through which to understand all social uses of mobile communications technologies. As a lens, mobile resourcefulness encourages us to look away from the technology per se – that is, from looking at one platform to understand how and why people are using it in particular ways – towards an approach which aims to identify and explore the wider social and communicative practices and individual needs that shape any one instance of technology use. As a starting point, the case studies in our book illustrate how resourcefulness underlies and shapes all situated uses of technology, although it manifests in different ways for different users. For example, some of our participants might be described as more experienced and confident technology users than others, and thus might appear to be more resourceful, at least in the lay sense of an innate ability to exploit resources (see Chapter 1). However, our argument is that each individual's resourcefulness lies in whatever technologically mediated practices enable them to achieve their purposes and perform their social identities, tech savvy or otherwise. We observed Marta, for example, to engage in a range of mobile practices alongside those already documented in this book (such as sending location data), including tethering (using her smartphone to connect her computer to the internet), recording and editing audio and video clips, taking screenshots, synchronising her calendar between her laptop and her phone, and actively using a range of mobile apps, including social media. She had a clear understanding of the importance of social media presence for her work as an artist and performer, and frequently posted on Facebook, Twitter and Tumblr information about her artistic activity, performances she attended or produced and her achievements. Marta was aware that using *mentions* and *hashtags* would make her posts searchable and allow people to participate in conversations related to the same themes. Thanks to this practice, Marta was able to be present in the online world and be part of arts-related discourse in London and beyond. She maintained connections also with the Polish arts scene, for example by posting information about a film festival in Gdańsk, and kept in touch with potential collaborators and contacts via email. In general, we can describe Marta as resourcefully and proficiently drawing on elements of her polymedia repertoire in promoting her work and becoming a hub for artists, including those in Poland and with a Polish connection, a mission she assigned to herself.

In comparison to Marta, Winnie was not an expert or prolific user of mobile phone communication or social media. As mentioned in Chapter 3, her uptake of new technology was facilitated and structured to some extent by her son, who passed his iPhone 4 down to her and set up a family WhatsApp group when his sister travelled to South Africa. Winnie's use of digital technologies was relatively limited. At work, she used the library's computer lending system and email with colleagues, but locked her mobile phone in her desk drawer, following the library's regulations. Outside work, she did not spend much time on her phone and she did not use social media sites such as Facebook or Instagram, perhaps because of other demands on her time as a working mother. Her personal and social use of SMS and WhatsApp could be described largely as that of micro-ordination, a use that Ling and Yttri (2002) identify as usually preceding a more emotional, interpersonal use. Nonetheless, Winnie could be seen to exploit the opportunity provided by messaging apps to enact and extend her existing social roles, manage her social activities, and enact personal values which were in turn shaped by her personal and cultural background, her migratory history, and her daily experiences at work. Winnie's emerging polymedia repertoire was clearly structured around her social relationships in distinct spheres of life. Across these spheres, in her mobile messages, we saw the remediation of a somewhat formal written style associated with personal letters, a style which reflects Winnie's wider beliefs in politeness and language use. We also saw a potential shift in Winnie's practices, as she selectively accommodated to her interlocutors' writing styles and learnt new 'txtspk' abbreviations, which facilitated an extension of her social relationships as she negotiated her online parenting role. Her apparently less confident use of mobile technology emerged from a complex set of social and personal circumstances and was shaped by her resourcefulness in drawing on its affordances to accomplish goals related to her wider values, relationships and social roles.

Similarly, users' resourcefulness is not constrained by consideration of how many apps and platforms make up their polymedia repertoire. Most of our participants – Edyta, Joe, Marta and Winnie – used a range of media, including social media and email alongside multiple mobile messaging apps. In contrast, those from mainland China relied much more on one app, namely WeChat. Like Facebook and Google, WeChat acts as a kind of 'walled garden' within the wider internet – that is, an online space which controls users' access to the web – with many users exclusively accessing the internet through the app. For example, we have seen how WeChat encompasses e-business opportunities and news-sharing facilities, as well as the ability to send written texts, audio recordings, images and memes. This diversification of communicative function is accompanied by a growing range of ways in which language and other resources are drawn upon, highlighting the fact that language use is shaped not by the technological constraints or any inherent features of the technology, but by however its users choose to use it. The ways in which Joanne and her interlocutors navigate the affordances of WeChat suggest that the app can itself be seen as a polymedia environment: an environment of different affordances which users navigate according to their communicative needs. In the same way as choosing to use WeChat is in itself a potentially meaningful act, choices made between various modes of communication available through the app are likely to be socially meaningful. Although we did not explore this directly, the fact that Joanne and her husband use the mobile messaging function to 'check in' with each other may mean that they are likely to interpret each other's typed messages as lacking urgency and having a primarily phatic function, and we might speculate what a phone call would mean in comparison. Joanne's line manager at work sent both written and audio messages, leading to questions around the difference in their status in comparison to written messages. In this sense, then, Madianou's (2014) argument that the smartphone should be seen as a polymedia environment can also be made with more specific reference to super-apps like WeChat. That is, WeChat, like the mobile phone, is both part of a wider polymedia environment and a polymedia environment itself. From our perspective, it is a complex resource within a polymedia repertoire, shaping the use of numerous embedded channels, modes and signs.

Concluding Remarks on Resourcefulness and Everyday Resistance

Resourcefulness is not a special property of some individuals or uses, but a feature of all technology use. Recognising that the principle of resourcefulness underlies people's use of technologies refocuses attention from the changes and novelties often seen to be brought about by new technologies towards continuities in human behaviour and the remediation of existing communicative practices. It also focuses attention on the *agency* of the technology user – on people's own articulated communicative purposes, self-positioning and social needs – and flags up the extent to which technology users can resist being passively positioned by the technology they use. Contemporary communications technologies often work to constrain and determine users' behaviour in ways that are economically valuable to the technology companies and advertisers, pushing data onto us, distracting us with incendiary or extreme views, rewarding us for clicking and for sharing, and determining the resources and functionalities available for social interaction (Jones and Hafner 2021). Resourcefulness in this sense is a form of everyday *resistance* by which people can push back at these constraints and performatively assert their own will. The way in which Kang Chen received meat orders through WeChat messaging, for example, challenges dominant ideas as to what mobile messaging is for, namely quasi-synchronous social chat (Tagg 2012). In contrast to much of what we know about mobile messaging, Kang Chen's messages were characterised by a dense, technical, business-related vocabulary and, rather than exploiting the app's affordance for instantaneous replies, he and the Chinese restaurant owners drew on the potential for asynchronicity and a permanent written record. We can also argue that the ways in which multimedia resources (such as weblinks, locations and photos) were offered to interlocutors through mobile messaging constitute an everyday exploitation of the available affordances for interpersonal ends in ways that go beyond the functions intended by social media companies. While inviting responses and social contact, through these acts of sharing or display, users acknowledge the particular conditions that characterise mobile messaging, the multiplicity of contexts invoked, and the multiple demands for their interlocutors' attention, and as such challenge the social media imperative to be constantly available.

Such ordinary acts of resistance are not necessarily conscious or ideologically informed, and neither are they necessarily pursued consistently. Users can also be complicit with commercial companies and dominant discourses – as when Joanne took up the commercial opportunity offered by WeChat Store – and their acts of resistance alternate with 'accommodative tendencies' (Canagarajah and Dovchin 2019: 128; see also Dovchin 2019). This 'untheorised, spontaneous and intuitive everyday resistance' (Canagarjah and Dovchin 2019: 142) is – as we saw with Kang Chen's meat orders – contained and constrained within a nexus of social, economic and political forces, our own habitus or historical bodies, and the people, artefacts, technologies and discourses around us. People are not, then, generally free to use their mobile phones in arbitrary or random ways, but they are able – as shown throughout this book – to harness the perceived affordances of a technology to the particularities of their context and, in so doing, accept, exploit or sometimes challenge how they are positioned to behave by social media companies and other actors. Importantly, as suggested above, this is not to say that people can always accurately assess the appropriateness of a particular technology for others in a particular context, or its effectiveness for a particular purpose. Neither can we say that being resourceful always 'works out' or is straightforwardly beneficial for all involved – as we saw when Edyta's customers started messaging her out of work hours. But looking at the uptake of mobile technologies in terms of mobile resourcefulness helps to foreground both the role of new technologies as semiotic resources and the distributed agency of the human within the context of dynamic, historically contingent, socioculturally situated and technologically mediated communicative spaces.

References

Abrams, J., J. O'Connor and H. Giles (2002) Identity and intergroup communication. In Gudykunst, W.B. and B. Mody (eds) *Handbook of International and Intercultural Communication*. London: Sage, pp. 225–240.

Adami, E. (2014) Retwitting, Reposting, Repinning; Reshaping Identities Online: Towards a Social Semiotic Multimodal Analysis of Digital Remediation. *LEA - Lingue e Lett. d'Oriente e d'Occidente* 3, 223–243. https://doi.org/10.13128/LEA-1824-484x-15194

Adami, E. (2009) 'We/YouTube': exploring sign-making in video-interaction. *Visual Communication* 8/4: 379–399.

Ahearn, L.M. (2010) Agency and language. In Jaspers, J., J.-O. Östman and J. Verschueren (eds) *Society and Language Use*. Amsterdam: John Benjamins, pp. 28–48.

Al Rashdi, F. (2018) Functions of emojis in WhatsApp interaction among Omanis. *Discourse, Context & Media* 26: 117–126.

Albawardi, A. (2018) The translingual digital practices of Saudi females on WhatsApp. *Discourse, Context & Media* 25: 68–77.

Al-Khatib, M. and E.H. Sabbah (2008) Language choice in mobile text messages among Jordanian university students. *Sky Journal of Linguistics* 21: 37–65.

Androutsopoulos, J. (2008) Potentials and limitations of discourse-centred online ethnography. *Language@Internet* 5, article 9.

Androutsopoulos, J. (2010) Localising the global on the participatory web. In Coupland, N. (ed.) *The Handbook of Language and Globalisation*. Oxford: Wiley-Blackwell, pp. 203–231.

Androutsopoulos, J. (2014) Moments of sharing: entextualisation and linguistic repertoires in social networking. *Journal of Pragmatics* 73: 4–18.

Androutsopoulos, J. (2015) Networked multilingualism: some language practices on Facebook and their implications. *International Journal of Bilingualism* 19/2: 185–205.

Androutsopoulos, J. (2021) Investigating digital language/media practices, awareness and pedagogy: introduction. *Linguistics and Education* 62: Article 100872.

Androutsopoulos, J. and A. De Fina (2021) Migrants/refugees and digital connectivity: sociolinguistic perspectives. Panel at Sociolinguistics Symposium 23, The University of Hong Kong, 7–10 June.

Androutsopoulos, J. and K. Juffermans (2014) Digital language practices in superdiversity: introduction. *Discourse, Context & Media* 4/5: 1–6.

Androutsopoulos, J. and A. Staehr (2017) Moving methods online: researching digital language practices. In Creese, A. and A. Blackledge (eds) *The Routledge Handbook of Language and Superdiversity: An Interdisciplinary Perspective*, pp. 118–132.

Appadurai, A. (1996) *Modernity at Large: Cultural Dimensions of Globalisation*. Minneapolis, MN: UMP.

Arminen, I. (2006) Social functions of location in mobile telephony. *Personal and Ubiquitous Computing* 10/5: 319–323.

Au, W.J. (2008) *The Making of Second Life: Notes from the New World*. New York: Collins.

Baron, N. (2000) *From Alphabet to Email: How Written Language Evolved and Where It's Heading*. London: Routledge.

Baron, N.S. (2010) Discourse structures in instant messaging: the case of utterance breaks. Language@Internet 7. Available: https://www.languageatinternet.org/articles/2010/2651 (accessed 03/02/2022).

Baron, N.S. (1998) Letters by phone or speech by other means: the linguistics of email. *Lang. Commun.* 18, 133–170.

Bax, S. (2011) Normalisation revisited: the effective use of technology in language education. *International Journal of Computer-Assisted Language Learning and Teaching* 1/2: 1–15.

Baym, N.K. (1993) Interpreting soap operas and creating community: inside a computer-mediated fan culture. *Journal of Folklore Research* 30/2–3: 143–177.

Beißwenger, M. (2008) Situated chat analysis as a window to the user's perspective: aspects of temporal and sequential organization. *Language@Internet* 5: 1–19.

Berry, D.M. and M. Dieter (2015) *Postdigital Aesthetics: Art, Computation and Design*. London: Palgrave.

Bezemer, J. and G. Kress (2017) Young people, Facebook, and pedagogy: recognising contemporary forms of multimodal text making. In Kontopodis, M., C. Varvantakis and C. Wulf (eds) *Global Youth in Digital Trajectories*. Abingdon: Routledge, pp. 22–38.

Bhattacharya, K. (2007) Consenting to the consent form: What are the fixed and fluid understandings between the researcher and researched? *Qualitative Inquiry* 13/8: 1095–1115.

Blackledge, A. and A. Creese (2018) Interaction ritual and the body in a city meat market. *Social Semiotics* 30/1: 1–24.

Blackledge, A., A. Creese and R. Hu (2015) Voice and social relations in a city market. *Working Papers in Translanguaging and Translation* (WP. 2). Available: https://tlang.org.uk/working-papers/ (accessed 07/04/21).

Blackledge, A., A. Creese and R. Hu (2016) Protean heritage, everyday superdiversity. *Working Papers in Translanguaging and Translation* (WP. 13). Available: https://tlang.org.uk/working-papers/ (accessed 07/04/21).

Blackledge, A., A. Creese and R. Hu (2017) Translanguaging, volleyball, and social life. *Working Papers in Translanguaging and Translation* (WP. 19). Available: https://tlang.org.uk/working-papers/ (accessed 07/04/21).

Blackledge, A., A. Creese and R. Hu (2018) Translating the city. *Working Papers in Translanguaging and Translation* (WP. 34). Available: https://tlang.org.uk/working-papers/ (accessed 07/04/21).

Blommaert, J. (2010) *Sociolinguistics of Globalization.* Cambridge: Cambridge University Press.

Boellstorff, T.B. (2008) *Coming of Age in Second Life: An Anthropologist Explores the Virtually Human.* Princeton, NJ: Princeton University Press.

Bolander, B. and M. Locher (2020) Beyond the online offline distinction: entry points to digital discourse. *Discourse, Context and Media* 35: Article 100383.

Bolter, J.D. and R. Grusin (2000) *Remediation: Understanding New Media.* Cambridge, M.A. MIT Press.

Bourdieu, P. (1977) *Outline of a Theory of Practice.* Cambridge: Cambridge University Press.

boyd, d.m. (2008) *Taken Out of Context: American Teen Sociality in Networked Publics.* Berkeley, CA: University of California Unpublished PhD thesis.

boyd, d.m. (2012) Networked privacy. *Surveillance and Society* 10(3–4): 348–350.

boyd, d.m. (2014) Making sense of teen life: strategies for capturing ethnographic data in a networked era. In Hargittai, E. and C. Sandvig (eds) *Digital Research Confidential: The Secrets of Studying Behavior Online.* Cambridge, MA: The MIT Press.

boyd, D.M. and N.B. Ellison (2008) Social network sites: definition, history, and scholarship. *Journal of Computer-Mediated Communication* 13: 210–230.

Busch, B. (2014) Building on heteroglossia and heterogeneity: the experience of a multilingual classroom. In Blackledge, A. and A. Creese (eds) *Heteroglossia as Practice and Pedagogy.* London: Springer, pp. 21–40.

Busch, F. (2021) The interactional principle in digital punctuation. *Discourse, Context & Media* 40: 100481.

Callaghan, J., E. Moore and J. Simpson (2018) Coordinated action, communication, and creativity in basketball in superdiversity. *Language and Intercultural Communication* 18/1: 28–53.

Canagarajah, S. and S. Dovchin (2019) The everyday politics of translingualism as a resistant practice. *International Journal of Multilingualism* 16/2: 127–144.

Carter, R. (2004) *Language and Creativity: the art of common talk.* Abingdon: Routledge.

Canale, M. and M. Swain (1980) Theoretical bases of communicative approaches to second language teaching and testing. *Applied Linguistics* 1/1: 1–47.

Chen, T. and M.-Y. Kan (2013) Creating a live, public short message service corpus: the NUS SMS corpus. *Language Resources and Evaluation* 47/2: 299–355.

Chen, Z., X. Lu, S. Shen, W. Ai, X. Liu and Q. Mei (2017) Through a gender lens: learning usage patterns of emojis from large-scale Android users. *WWW '18: Proceedings of the 2018 World Wide Web Conference,* April 2018, pp. 763–772.

Chiluwa, I. (2008) Assessing the Nigerianness of SMS text-messages in English. *English Today* 24/1: 51–56.

Church, K. and R. de Oliveira (2013) What's up with WhatsApp? Comparing mobile instant messaging with traditional SMS. Proceedings of *Mobile HCI 2013: Collaboration and Communication*, Munich, Germany, 27–30 August 2013.

Clifford, James (1997) *Routes: Travel and Translation in the Late Twentieth Century*. Cambridge, MA: Harvard University Press.

Cohen, L. (2015) World attending in interaction: multitasking, spatializing, narrativizing with mobile devices and Tinder. *Discourse, Context and Media* 9: 46–54.

Collie, P., S. Kindon, J. Liu and A. Podsiadlowski (2010) Mindful identity negotiations: The acculturation of young Assyrian women in New Zealand. *International Journal of Intercultural Relations* 34/3: 208–220.

Collins, M. and R. Thompson (2020) Disruptive practice: multimodality, innovation and standardisation from the medieval to the digital text. In Tagg, C. and M. Evans (eds) *Message and Medium: English Language Practices across Old and New Media*. Berlin: De Gruyter Mouton, pp. 281–305.

Corbett, A.C. and J.A. Katz (2003) *Entrepreneurial Resourcefulness: competing with constraints*. Bingley: Emerald Group Publishing.

Cramer, F. (2014) What is 'post-digital'? *ARRJA* 3/1: 11–24.

Creese, A. and A. Blackledge (2011) Separate and flexible bilingualism in complementary schools: multiple language practices in interrelationship. *Journal of Pragmatics* 43/5: 1196–1208.

Creese, A. and A. Blackledge (2019) Translanguaging and public service encounters: language learning in the library. *Modern Language Journal* 103/4: 800–814.

Crider, J.A. and S. Ganesh (2004) Negotiating meaning in virtual teams: context, roles and computer mediated communication in college classrooms. In Godar, S.H. and S.P. Ferris (eds) *Virtual and Collaborative Teams: Process, Technologies and Practice*. Hershey: Idea Group, pp. 133–155.

Crystal, D. (2001) *Language and the Internet*. Cambridge: Cambridge University Press.

Danet, B. (2001) *Cyberpl@y: Communicating Online*. Oxford: Berg Publishers.

DCMS (2018) House of Commons Digital, Culture, Media and Sport Committee Disinformation and 'fake news': final report. 14 February 2019. Available: https://publications.parliament.uk/pa/cm201719/cmselect/cmcumeds/1791/179102.htm (accessed 07/04/2021).

Deng, I. and C. Chen (2018) How WeChat became China's everyday mobile app. *South China Morning Post*, 16 August 2018.

Depperman, A. and J. Streeck (2018) *Time in Embodied Interaction: Synchronicity and Sequentiality of Multimodal Resources*. Amsterdam: John Benjamins.

Deumert, A. and S.O. Masinyana (2008) Mobile language choices – the use of English and isiXhosa in text messages (SMS) evidence from a bilingual South African sample. *English World-Wide* 29/2: 117–147.

Dewulf, A., B. Gray, L. Putnam, R. Lewicki, N. Aarts, R. Bouwen and C. van Woerkum (2009) Disentangling approaches to framing in conflict and negotiation research: a meta-paradigmatic perspective. *Human Relations* 62: 155–193.

Djonov, E. and T. van Leeuwen (2017) The power of semiotic software: a critical multimodal perspective. In J. Flowerdew and J.E. Richardson (eds) *The Routledge Handbook of Critical Discourse Studies*. Abingdon: Routledge, pp. 566–581.

Djonov, E. and T. van Leeuwen (2018) Social media as semiotic technology and social practice: the case of ResearchGate's design and its potential to transform social practice. *Social Semiotics* 28/5: 641–664.

Domingo, M. (2014) Transnational language flows in digital platforms: a study of urban youth and their multimodal text making. *Pedagogies* 9/1: 7–25.

Dovchin, S. (2019) Language crossing and linguistic racism: Mongolian immigrant women in Australia. *Journal of Multicultural Discourses* 14/4: 334–351.

Dovchin, S., A. Pennycook and S. Sultana (2018) *Popular Culture, Voice and Linguistic Diversity: young adults on- and offline*. Cham, Switzerland: Palgrave.

Ducheneaut, N. (2010) The chorus of the dead: roles, identity formation, and ritual processes inside an FPS Multiplayer Online Game. In J.T. Wright, D.G. Embrick and A. Lukács (eds) *Utopic Dreams and Apocalyptic Fantasies: Critical Approaches to Researching Video Game Play*. Plymouth: Lexington Books, pp. 199–222.

Duggan, M. (2017) Questioning 'digital ethnography' in an era of ubiquitous computing. *Geography Compass*. 11/5: 1–12. Published March 2017.

Duranti, A. (2006) Agency in language. In Duranti, A. (ed.) *A Companion to Linguistic Anthropology*. Oxford: Blackwell, pp. 451–473.

Dürscheid, C. (2016) Neue Dialoge – alte Konzepte? [New dialogues – old concepts?]. *Zeitschrift Für Germanistische Linguistik* 44(3): 437–468.

Dürscheid, C. and E. Stark (2011) SMS4science: An international corpus-based texting project and the specific challenges for multilingual Switzerland. In Thurlow, C. and K. Mroczek (eds) *Digital Discourse. Language in the New Media*. Oxford: Oxford University Press, pp. 299–320.

Evans, M. and C. Tagg (2021) Women's spelling in early modern English: perspectives from new media. In Condorelli, M. (ed.) *Advances in Historical Orthography, c. 1500–1800*. Cambridge: Cambridge University Press, pp. 191–218.

Fairon, C. and S. Paumier (2006) *A Translated Corpus of 30,000 French SMS*. Geneva: LREC.

Galani-Moutafi, V. (2000) The self and the other: traveller, ethnographer, tourist. *Annals of Tourism Research* 27/1: 203–224.

Gallardo, R. and M. Wiltse (2018) *Gauging Household Digital Readiness*. December 2018. Purdue University. West Lafayette, I.N.

Garcia, A.C. and J. Baker Jacobs (1999) The eyes of the beholder: understanding the turn-taking system in quasi-synchronous computer-mediated communication. *Research on Language & Social Interaction* 32: 337–367.

Ge, J. and S.C. Herring (2019) Communicative functions of emoji sequences on Sina Weibo. *First Monday* 23/11.

Geertz, C. (1973) *The Interpretation of Cultures*. New York: Basic Books.

Georgakopoulou, A. (2017) 'Friendly' comments: interactional displays of alignment on Facebook and YouTube. In Leppanen, S., E. Westinen and S. Kytola (eds) *Social Media Discourse, (Dis)identifications and Diversities.* Abingdon: Routledge, pp. 179–207.

Georgalou, M. (2017) *Discourse and Identity on Facebook.* London: Bloomsbury.

Gershon, I. (2010) *The Breakup 2.0.* Ithaca, NY: Cornell University Press.

Giddens, A. (1979) *Central Problems in Social Theory: Action, Structure and Contradiction in Social Analysis.* Berkeley, CA: University of California Press.

Giles, D., W. Stommel and Paulus, T.M. (2017) Introduction: the microanalysis of online data: the next stage. *Journal of Pragmatics* 115: 37–41.

Giles, D., W. Stommel, T. Paulus, J. Lester and Reed, D. (2015) Microanalysis Of Online Data: the methodological development of 'digital CA'. *Discourse, Context & Media* 7: 45–51.

Gitelman, L. (2006) *Always Already New: Media, History, and the Data of Culture.* Cambridge, MA: MIT Press.

Goffman, E. (1967) *Interaction Ritual: Essays on Face-to-Face Interaction.* Chicago, IL: Aldine.

Goffman, E. (1974) *Frame Analysis: An Essay on the Organization of Experience.* New York: Harper Row.

Gomes, C. (2018) *Siloed Diversity: Transnational Migration, Digital Media and Social Networks.* London: Palgrave.

Goodson, L. and C. Tagg (2017) Working in large diverse teams to explore superdiversity. In Creese, A. and A. Blackledge (eds) *The Routledge Handbook of Language and Superdiversity.* Abingdon: Routledge, pp. 103–117.

Gumperz, J. (1964) Linguistic and social interaction in two communities. *American Anthropologist* 66: 137–53.

Gumperz, J. (1999) On interactional sociolinguistic method. In S. Sarangi and C. Roberts (eds) *Talk, Work and Institutional Order.* Berlin: Mouton, pp. 453–71.

Gumperz, J. and D. Hymes (eds) (1972) *Directions in Sociolinguistics: The Ethnography of Communication.* Oxford: Blackwell.

Haggan, M. (2007) Text messaging in Kuwait. Is the medium the message? *Multilingua* 26: 427–449.

Hammersley, M. and P. Atkinson (1995) *Ethnography.* London: Routledge.

Hard af Segerstad, Y. (2002) *Use and Adaptation of the Written Language to the Conditions of Computer-mediated Communication.* Götěborg: University of Götěborg, PhD Thesis.

Hendus, U. (2015) 'See Translation': explicit and implicit language policies on Facebook. *Language Policy* 14: 397–417.

Herring, S.C. (2004) Computer-mediated discourse analysis: an approach to researching online behavior. In Barab, S.A., R. Kling and J.H. Gray (eds) *Designing for Virtual Communities in the Service of Learning.* New York: Cambridge University Press, pp. 338–376.

Herring, S.C. (2007) A faceted classification scheme for computer-mediated discourse. *Language@Internet* 4: article 1. Retrieved from: https://www.languageatinternet.org/articles/2007/761.

Herring, S.C. (2018) The coevolution of computer-mediated communication and computer-mediated discourse analysis. In Bou-Franch, P. and G.-C. Blitvich (eds) *Analyzing Digital Discourse: New Insights and Future Directions*. London: Palgrave, pp. 25–67.

Herring, S.C. and A. Dainas (2017) 'Nice picture comment!' Graphicons in Facebook comment threads. Proceedings of the 50th Hawaii International Conference on System Sciences, pp. 2185–2194.

Herring, S.C., A.R. Dainas, H. Lopez Long and Y. Tang (2020) Animoji performances: 'cuz I can be a sexy poop'. *Language@Internet* 18: Article 1.

Heyd, T. (2014) Doing race and ethnicity in a digital community: lexical labels and narratives of belonging in a Nigerian web forum. *Discourse, Context & Media* 4/5: 38–47.

Hillewart, S. (2015) Writing with an accent: orthographic practice, emblems and traces on Facebook. *Linguistic Anthropology* 25/2: 195–214.

Hine, C. (2000) *Virtual Ethnography*. London: Sage.

Hjorth, L., K. Ohashi, J. Sinanan, H. Horst, S. Pink, F. Kato and B. Zhou (2020) *Digital Media Practices in Households: kinship through data*. Amsterdam University Press: Amsterdam.

Hockey, J. (2002) Interviews as ethnography? Disembodied social interaction in Britain. In Rapport, N. (ed.) *British Subjects: An Anthropology of Britain*. Oxford: Berg.

Hsieh, S.H. and T.H. Tseng (2017) Playfulness in mobile instant messaging: examining the influence of emoticons and text messaging on social interaction. *Computers in Human Behavior* 69: 405–414.

Hua, Z., L. Wei and A. Lyons (2015) Language, business and superdiversity in London: Translanguaging business. *Working Papers in Translanguaging and Translation* (WP. 5). Available: https://tlang.org.uk/working-papers/ (accessed 07/04/21).

Hua, Z., L. Wei and A. Lyons (2015) Language, business and superdiversity in London: Translanguaging Business. *Working Papers in Translanguaging and Translation* (WP. 5). Available: https://tlang.org.uk/working-papers/ (accessed 07/04/21).

Hua, Z., L. Wei and A. Lyons (2016) Playful subversiveness and creativity: Doing a/n (Polish) artist in London. *Working Papers in Translanguaging and Translation* (WP. 16). Available: https://tlang.org.uk/working-papers/ (accessed 07/04/21).

Hua, Z., L. Wei and A. Lyons (2017) Polish shop(ping) as translanguaging space. *Social Semiotics* 27/4: 411–433.

Hua, Z., L. Wei and D. Jankowicz-Pytel (2017) Translating culture in multilingual karate in London. *Working Papers in Translanguaging and Translation* (WP20). Available: https://tlang.org.uk/working-papers/ (accessed 07/04/21).

Hua, Z., L. Wei and D. Jankowicz-Pytel (2018) Intercultural moments in translating the socio-legal systems. *Working Papers in Translanguaging and Translation* (WP. 35) Available: https://tlang.org.uk/working-papers/ (accessed 07/04/21).

Hymes, D.H. (1978) *What is Ethnography?* Southwest Educational Development Laboratory.

Ilbury, C. (2019) 'Sassy queens': stylistic orthographic variation and the enregisterment of AAVE. *Journal of Sociolinguistics* 24: 245–264.

Ito, M. et al. (2010) *Hanging Out, Messing Around and Geeking Out: kids living and learning with new media*. Cambridge, MA: MIT Press.

Janssen, J.H., W.A. Ijsselsteijn and J.H.D.M. Westerink (2014) How affective technologies can influence intimate interactions and improve social connectedness. *International Journal of Human-Computer Studies* 72/1: 33–43.

John, N.A. (2017) *The Age of Sharing*. Cambridge: Polity Press.

Johnson, A. (2011) *A Brief History of Diaries: From Pepys to Blogs*. London: Hesperus Press.

Jones, R.H. (2008) The role of text in televideo cybersex. *Text & Talk* 28/4: 453–473.

Jones, R.H. (2010) Cyberspace and physical space: attention structures in computer mediated communication. In Jaworski, A. and C. Thurlow (eds) *Cyberspace and Physical Space: Attention Structures in Computer Mediated Communication*. London: Continnum, pp. 151–167.

Jones, R.H. (2020) Towards an embodied visual semiotics: negotiating the right to look. In Thurlow, C., C. Dürscheid and F. Diémoz (eds) *Visualising Digital Discourse: Interactional, Insitutional and Ideological Perspectives*. Berlin: De Gruyter Mouton, pp. 19–42.

Jones, R.H. and C. Hafner (2012) *Digital Literacies: A Practical Introduction*. 1st edn. Abingdon: Routledge.

Jones, R.H. and C.A. Hafner (2021) *Digital Literacies: A Practical Introduction*. 2nd edn. Abingdon: Routledge.

Jones, T. (2016) Tweets as graffiti: what the reconstruction of Vulgar Latin can tell us about Black Twitter. In Squires, L. (ed.) *English in Computer-Mediated Communication: Variation, Representation and Change*. Berlin: De Gruyter Mouton, pp. 43–68.

Jonsson, K. and A. Muhonen (2014) Multilingual repertoires and the relocalization of manga in digital media. *Discourse, Context & Media* 4/5: 87–100.

Karrebæk, M.S., A. Stæhr and P. Varis (2014) Punjabi at heart: Language, legitimacy, and authenticity on social media. *Discourse, Context & Media* 8: 20–29.

Katz, J. and M. Aakhus (2002) *Perpetual Contact: Mobile Communication, Private Talk, Public Performance*. Cambridge: Cambridge University Press

Keefe, P.R. (2009) Snakeheads and smuggling: the dynamics of illegal Chinese immigration *World Policy Journal* 26/1: 33–44.

Kelty, C.M. (2008) *Two Bits: The Cultural Significance of Free Software*. Durham, NC: Duke University Press.

Kendall, L. (2002) *Hanging Out in the Virtual Pub: Masculinities and Relationships Online*. Berkeley, CA: University of California Press.

König, K. (2019) Sequential patterns in SMS and WhatsApp dialogues: practices for coordinating actions and managing topics. *Discourse & Communication* 13/6: 612–629.

Konrad, A., S.C. Herring and D. Choi (2020) Sticker and emoji use in Facebook Messenger: implications for graphicon change. *Journal of Computer-Mediated Communication* 25: 217–235.

Kozinets, R. (2009) *Netnography: Doing Ethnographic Research Online*, Thousand Oaks: SAGE Publications Ltd.

Kozinets, R.V. (2010) *Netnography: Doing Ethnographic Research Online*. London: Sage Publications.

Kress, G. (2010) *Multimodality: A Social Semiotic Approach to Communication*. London: Routledge.

Kress, G. and T. van Leeuwen (1996) *Reading Images: the grammar of visual design*, 1st edition. Abingdon: Routledge.

Kubanyiova, M. (2008) Rethinking research ethics in contemporary applied linguistics: The tension between macroethical and microethical perspectives in situated research. *Modern Language Journal* 92/4: 503–518.

Kuijer, L., I. Nicenboim and E. Giaccardi (2017) Conceptualising resourcefulness as a dispersed practice. *DIS 17 Proceedings of the 2017 Conference on Designing Interactive Systems*, pp. 15–27.

Kusters, A., M. Spotti, R. Swanwick and E. Tapio (2017) Beyond languages, beyond modalities: transforming the study of semiotic repertoires. *International Journal of Multilingualism* 14/3: 219–232.

Kytölä, S. and J. Androutsopoulos (2012) Ethnographic perspectives on multilingual computer-mediated discourse: insights from Finnish football forums on the web. In Gardner, S. and M. Martin-Jones (eds) *Multilingualism, Discourse and Ethnography*. Abingdon: Routledge, pp. 179–917.

Laitinen, K. and M. Valo (2018) Meanings of communication technology in virtual team meetings: framing technology-related interaction. *International Journal of Human-Computer Studies* 111: 12–22.

Laurenceau, J.P., L.F. Barrett and P.R. Pietromonaco (1998) Intimacy as an interpersonal process: the importance of self-disclosure, partner disclosure, and perceived partner responsiveness in interpersonal exchanges. *Journal of Personality and Social Psychology* 74: 1238–1251.

Laursen, D. and M.H. Szymanski (2013) Where are you? Location talk in mobile phone conversations. *Mobile Media & Communication* 1/3: 314–334.

Lee, C. (2007) Affordances and text-making practices in online instant messaging. *Written Communication* 24/3: 223–249.

Lee, C. (2011) Texts and practices of micro-blogging: status updates on Facebook. In Thurlow, C. and K. Mroczek (eds) *Digital Discourse: language in new media*. Oxford: Oxford University Press, pp. 110–128.

Lee, C. (2014) Language choice and self-presentation in social media: the case of university students in Hong Kong. In Seargeant, P. and C. Tagg (eds) *The Language of Social Media: Identity and Community on the Internet*. London: Palgrave, pp. 91–111.

Lenihan, A. (2014) Investigating language policy in social media: translation practices on Facebook. In Seargeant, P. and C. Tagg (eds) *The Language of Social Media: Identity and Community on the Internet*. London: Palgrave, pp. 208–227.

Leppänen, S. and A. Elo (2015) Buffalaxing the other: superdiversity in action on YouTube. In Arnaut, K., J. Blommaert, B. Rampton and M. Spotti (eds) *Language and Superdiversity*. London: Routledge, pp. 110–136.

Leppänen, S., S. Kytola, H. Jousmaki, S. Peuronen and E. Westinen (2014) Entextualisation and resemiotization as resources for identification in social media. In Seargeant, P. and C. Tagg (eds) *The Language of Social Media: Identity and Community on the Internet*. London: Palgrave, pp. 112–136.

Leurs, K. and K. Smets (2018) Five questions for digital migration studies: learning from digital connectivity and forced migration in(to) Europe. *Social Media + Society* January-March, 4/1: 1–16.

Levin, S. (2017) Mark Zuckerberg: I regret ridiculing fears over Facebook's effect on election. *The Guardian* 28th September.

Lexander, K.V. (2011) Texting and African language literacy. *New Media & Society* 13/3: 427–443.

Lexander, K.V. and J. Androutsopoulos (2021) Working with mediagrams: a methodology for collaborative research on mediational repertoires in multilingual families. *Journal of Multilingual and Multicultural Development* 42/1: 1–18.

Liao, S. (2018) How WeChat came to rule China: the multipurpose messaging app is becoming the nation's ID system. *The Verge.* Feb 1, 2018.

Lillis, T. (2013) *The Sociolinguistics of Writing.* Edinburgh: Edinburgh University Press.

Ling, R. and B. Yttri (2002) Hyper-coordination via mobile phones in Norway. In Katz, J.E. and M. Aakhus (eds) *Perpetual Contact: Mobile Communication, Private Talk, Public Performance.* Cambridge, UK: Cambridge University Press, pp. 139–169.

Ling, R. and H.A. Horst (2011) Mobile communication in the global south. *New Media & Society* 13/3: 363–374.

Littlemore, J. and C. Tagg (2019) Metonymy and text messaging: a framework for understanding creative uses of metonymy. *Applied Linguistics* 39/4: 481–507.

Luega, J. (2020) The pragma-stylistics of 'image macro' internet memes (2020). In Ringrow, H. and S. Pihlaja (eds) *Contemporary Media Stylistics.* London: Bloomsbury, pp. 81–106.

Lundberg, C. and I. Gunn (2005) 'Ouija board, are there any communications?' Agency, ontotheology, and the death of the humanist subject, or, continuing the ARS conversation. *Rhetoric Society Quarterly* 35/4: 83–105.

Lyons, A. (2014) *Self-presentation and Self-positioning in Text-messages: Embedded Multimodality, Deixis, and Reference Frame.* London: School of Languages, Linguistics & Film, Queen Mary University of London PhD thesis.

Lyons, A. (2018) Multimodal expression in written digital discourse: the case of kineticons. *Journal of Pragmatics* 131: 18–29.

Lyons, A. (2020) Negotiating the expertise paradox in new mothers' WhatsApp group interactions. *Discourse, Context & Media* 37: Article 100427.

Lyons, A. and C. Tagg (2019) The discursive construction of mobile chronotopes in mobile-phone messaging. *Language in Society* 48/5: 657–683.

Lyons, A. and C. Tagg (2021) Post-digital connectivities: mobile messaging and intersemiotic translanguaging in culturally framing offline encounters. Sociolinguistics Symposium 23, The University of Hong Kong, 7–10 June.

Lyons, A. and S. Ounoughi (2020) Towards a transhistorical approach to analysing discourse about and in motion. In Tagg, C. and M. Evans (eds) *Message and Medium: English Language Practices across Old and New Media.* Berlin: de Gruyter Mouton, pp. 89–111.

Lyons, A., Tagg, C. and R. Hu (2019) Chronotopic (non)modernity in translocal mobile messaging among Chinese migrants in the UK. *Internet Pragmatics* 4/2: 190–218.

Mackenzie, J. (2017) *Language, Gender and Parenthood Online: Negotiating Motherhood in Mumsnet Talk.* London: Routledge.

Madianou, M. (2014) Smartphones as polymedia. *Journal of Computer-Mediated Communication* 19: 667–680.

Madianou, M. (2015) Polymedia and ethnography. *Social Media + Society* 1/1: 1–3.

Madianou, M. and D. Miller (2012) Polymedia: towards a new theory of digital media in interpersonal communication. *International Journal of Cultural Studies* 16/2: 169–187.

Madsen, L.M., M.S. Karrebæk and J.M. Møller (eds) (2016) *Everyday Languaging: Collaborative Research on the Language Use of Children and Youth*. Berlin: de Gruyter Mouton.

Maier, C.T. and D. Deluliis (2015) Recovering the human in the network: Exploring communicology in digital business discourse. In Darics, E. (ed.) *Digital Business Discourse*. London: Palgrave Macmillan, pp. 208–225.

Markham, A.N. and E. Buchanan (2015) Ethical considerations in digital research contexts. In Wright, J. (ed.) *Encyclopedia for Social & Behavioral Sciences*. Amsterdam: Elsevier Press, pp. 606–613.

Marsh, J. (2019) Researching young children's play in the post-digital age. In Kucirkova, N., J. Rowsell and G. Falloon (eds) *The Routledge International Handbook of Learning with Technology in Early Years*. Abingdon: Routledge.

Marvin, C. (1988) *When Old Technologies Were New: Thinking About Electric Communication in the Late Nineteenth Century*. Oxford: Oxford University Press.

Mauss, Marcel. (2002) *Essai sur le don*. First edition. Abingdon: Psychology Press.

Mavers, D. (2007) Semiotic resourcefulness: a young child's email exchange as design. *Journal of Early Childhood Literacy* 7/2: 155–176.

Maybin, J. and J. Swann (2007) Everyday creativity in language: textuality, contextuality, and critique. *Applied Linguistics* 28/4: 497–517.

McLaughlin, F. (2014) Senegalese digital repertoires in superdiversity: a case study from Seneweb. *Discourse, Context & Media* 4/5: 29–37.

McLuhan, M. (1964) *Understanding Media: The Extensions of Man*. New York: McGraw Hill.

Meiler, M. (2021) Story-telling in instant messenger communication: sequencing a story without turn-taking. *Discourse, Context & Media* 43: Article 100515.

Miller, D. (2016) *Social Media in an English Village*. London: UCL Press.

Miller, D. and J. Sinanan (2014) *Webcam*. Cambridge: Polity Press.

Miller, E.R. (2016) The ideology of learner agency and the nonliberal self. *International Journal of Applied Linguistics* 26/3: 348–365.

Milroy, L. (1987) *Language and Social Networks*. New York: Blackwell.

Mondada, L. (2018) The multimodal interactional organization of tasting: practices of tasting cheese in gourmet shops. *Discourse Studies* 20/6: 743–769.

Moores, S. (2004) The doubling of place: electronic media, time-space arrangements and social relationships. In Couldry, N. and A. McCarthy (eds) *MediaSpace: Place, Scale and Culture in a Media Age*. London: Routledge, pp. 21–36.

Morel, E., C. Bucher, S. Pekarek Doehler and B. Siebenhaar (2014) SMS communication as plurilingual communication: hybrid language as a challenge for classical code-switching categories. In L.-A. Cougnon and Fairon, C. (eds)

SMS Communication: a linguistic approach. Amsterdam: John Benjamins, pp. 111–140.

Morel, E., C. Bucher, S. Pekarek Doehler and B. Siebenhaar (2012) SMS communication as plurilingual communication: hybrid language use as a challenge for classical code-switching categories. *Linguisticae Investigationes* 35/2: 260–288.

Mosakowski, E. (2002) Overcoming resource disadvantages in entrepreneurial firms: when less is more. In Hitt, M.A., R.D. Ireland, S.M. Camp and D.L. Sexton (eds) *Strategic Entrepreneurship: Creating a New Mindset*. Oxford: Wiley Blackwell, pp. 106–126.

Narjes, C. (2018) Importance of being digital ready: what does that mean? *Cornhusker Economics*, September 12.

Nordquist, B. (2017) *Literacy and Mobility: Complexity, Uncertainty, and Agency at the Nexus of High School and College*. New York: Routledge.

OED (online) Oxford English dictionary. Available: https://www.oed.com/ (accessed 23/4/2021).

Orgad, S. (2009) How can researchers make sense of the issues involved in collecting and interpreting online and offline data? In A.N. Markham and N.K. Baym (eds) *Internet Inquiry: Conversations About Method*. Los Angeles: Sage, pp. 32–53.

Page, R., D. Barton, J.W. Unger and M. Zappavigna (2014) *Researching Language and Social Media: A Student Guide*. London: Routledge.

Panckhurst, R. and F. Frontini (2020) Evolving interactional practices of emoji in text messages. In Thurlow, C., C. Dürscheid and Diémoz (eds) *Visualising Digital Discourse: Interactional, Insitutional and Ideological Perspectives*. Berlin: De Gruyter Mouton, pp. 81–104.

Papacharissi, Z. (ed.) (2011) *A Networked Self: Identity, Community, and Culture on Social Network Sites*. London: Routledge.

Papen, U. (2005) *Adult Literacy as Social Practice: More Than Skills*. London: Routledge.

Parks, M.R. and K. Floyd (1996) Making friends in cyberspace. *Journal of Computer-Mediated Communication* 1/4.

Paulus, T., A. Warren and J.N. Lester (2016) Applying conversation analysis methods to online talk: a literature review. *Discourse, Context & Media* 12: 1–10.

Pennington, R. and J. Birthisel (2016) When new media makes news: framing technology and sexual assault in the Steubenville rape case. *New Media & Society* 18/11: 2435–2451.

Pennycook, A. (2018) Posthumanist applied linguistics. *Applied Linguistics* 39/4: 445–461.

Pennycook, A. and Otsuji, E. (2015) *Metrolingualism: Language in the City*. Abingdon: Routledge.

Pérez-Sabater, C. (2018) Emoticons in relational writing practices on WhatsApp: some reflections on gender. In Bou-Franch, P. and P. Garcés-Conejos Blitvich (eds) *Analyzing Digital Discourse: New Insights and Future Directions*. London: Palgrave, pp. 163–189.

Peuronen, S. (2011) 'Ride hard, live forever': translocal identities in an online community of extreme sports Christians. In Thurlow, C. and K. Mroczek (eds)

Digital Discourse: Language in the New Media. Oxford: Oxford University Press, pp. 154–176.

Pinnow, R.J. (2011) 'I've got an idea': a social semiotic perspective on agency in the second language classroom. *Linguistics and Education* 22: 383–392.

Piot, C. (1999) *Remotely Global: Village Modernity in West Africa.* Chicago: University of Chicago Press.

Herring, S.C. (2010) Computer-mediated conversation: introduction and overview. *Language@Internet* 7. Available: https://www.languageatinternet.org/articles/2010/2801 (accessed 03/02/2022).

Pohl, H., C. Domin and M. Rohs (2017) Beyond just text: semantic emoji similarity modeling to support expressive communication. *ACM Transactions on Computer-Human Interaction* 24/1: 1–42. Article 6.

Powel, E.E. and T. Baker (2011) Beyond making do: toward a theory of entrepreneurial resourcefulness. *Frontiers of Entrepreneurial Research* 31/12: 376–388.

Quan-Haase, A. and A.L. Young (2010) Uses and gratifications of social media: a comparison of Facebook and instant messaging. *Bulletin of Science, Technology & Society*, 30/5: 350–361.

Rampton, B., K. Tusting, J. Maybin, R. Barwell, A. Creese and V. Lytra (2004) Linguistic ethnography in the UK: A discussion paper. Available: http://www.lancaster.ac.uk/fss/organisations/lingethn/documents/discussion_paper_jan_05.pdf (accessed 27/11/2015).

Reid, E.M. (1991) *Electropolis: Communication and Community on Internet Relay Chat.* Master's Thesis. Melbourne, Australia: Department of History, University of Melbourne.

Reinsch, N.L., J.W. Turner and C.H. Tinsley (2008) Multicommunicating: a practice whose time has come? *The Academy of Management Review* 33/2: 391–403.

Rheingold, H. (1993) *The Virtual Community: Homesteading on the Electronic Frontier.* Reading, MA: Addison-Wesley.

Rymes, B. (2014) Marking communicative repertoire through metacommentary. In Blackledge, A. and A. Creese (eds) *Heteroglossia as Practice and Pedagogy.* London: Springer, pp. 301–316.

Schegloff, E.A. and H. Sacks (1973) Opening up closings. *Semiotica* 8/4: 289–327.

Scollon, R. (2001) *Mediating Discourse: The Nexus of Practice.* New York: Routledge.

Scollon, R. and S.W. Scollon (2004) *Nexus Analysis: Discourse and the Emerging Internet.* Abingdon: Routledge.

Sharapan, M. (2016) Tibetan cultural identity in Nepal: change, preservation, prospects. *Journal of Intercultural Communication* 45/5: 374–390.

Shortis, T. (2007) Revoicing Txt: spelling, vernacular orthography and "unregimented" writing. In Posteguillo, S., M.J. Esteve and M.L. Gea (eds) *The Texture of Internet: Netlinguistics.* Cambridge: Cambridge Scholar Press, pp. 2–21.

Shortis, T. (2016) Texting and other messaging: written system in digitally mediated vernaculars. In Cook, V. and D. Ryan (eds) *The Routledge Handbook of the English Writing System.* Abingdon: Routledge, pp. 487–511.

Siebenhaar, B. (2016) WhatsApp-Kommunikation: Ist der Gebrauch von Emojis altersspezifiziert? (WhatsApp communication: is the use of emoji age-specific?).

Talk given at the *Tagung Jugendsprachen 2016: Variation - Dynamik - Kontinuität*, Graz, 26 May.

Siever, C. (2016) Iconographetic communication in digital media: emojis in WhatsApp, Twitter, Instagram etc. Talk given at *Emoticons, Emoji and Kaomoji – The Transformation of Communication in the Digital Age* at the Freien Universität Berlin, 23 June.

Silverstein M. (1985) Language and the culture of gender: at the intersection of structure, usage and ideology. In Mertz, E. and R. Parmentier (eds) *Semiotic Mediation: Sociocultural and Psychological Perspectives*. New York: Academic Press, pp. 219–259.

Singh, J.N. (2016) *Transcultural Voices: Narrating Hip Hop Culture in Complex Delhi*. Unpublished PhD thesis, Cardiff: Cardiff University.

Skinner, J. (2012) *The Interview: An Ethnographic Approach*. Oxford: Berg.

Spilioti, T. (2011) Beyond genre: closings and relational work in text-messaging. In Thurlow, C. and K. Mroczek (eds) *Digital Discourse: Language in the New Media*. Oxford: Oxford University Press, pp. 67–85.

Spilioti, T. and C. Tagg (2017) The ethics of online research methods in applied linguistics: challenges, opportunities, and directions in ethical decision-making. *Applied Linguistics Review* 8/2–3: 163–167.

Spilioti, T. and C. Tagg (2022) Research ethics. In Vasquéz, C. (ed.) *Research Methods for Digital Discourse Analysis*. New York: Bloomsbury.

Spilioti, T. (2011) Beyond genre: closings and relational work in text-messaging. In Thurlow, C. and K. Mroczel (eds) *Digital Discourse: Language in the New Media*, Oxford Studies in Sociolinguistics, Oxford: Oxford University Press, pp. 67–85.

Stæhr, A. (2015) Reflexivity in Facebook interaction – enregisterment across written and spoken language practices. *Discourse, Context and Media* 8: 30–45.

Stæhr, A. (2016) Languaging and normativity on Facebook. In Arnaut, K., M. Spotti and M.S. Karrebæk (eds) *Engaging Superdiversity: Recombining Spaces, Times and Language Practices*. Bristol: Multilingual Matters, pp. 170–195.

Staehr, A.C. and T.R. Nørreby (2021) The metapragmatics of mode choice. *Pragmatics and Society* 12/5: 756–781.

Stommel, W., T.M. Paulus and D. Giles (2017) The microanalysis of online data: the next stage. *Journal of Pragmatics* 115: 37–41.

Sundén, J. (2003) *Material Virtualities: Approaching Online Textual Embodiment*. New York: Peter Lang.

Swann, J., A. Deumert, T. Lillis and R. Mesthrie (2004) *A Dictionary of Sociolinguistics*. Edinburgh: Edinburgh University Press.

Tagg, C. (2009) *A corpus linguistics study of SMS text messaging*. Unpubl. PhD thesis.

Tagg, C. (2012) *The Discourse of Text Messaging: Analysis of SMS Communication*. London: Continuum.

Tagg, C. (2013) Scraping the barrel with a shower of social misfits: everyday creativity in text messaging. *Applied Linguistics* 34/4: 480–500.

Tagg, C. (2015) Language, business and superdiversity: a report on social media across case studies. *Working Papers in Translanguaging and Translation* (WP6). Available: https://tlang.org.uk/working-papers/ (accessed 07/04/21).

Tagg, C. (2016) Heteroglossia in text-messaging: performing identity and negotiating relationships in a digital space. *Journal of Sociolinguistics* 20/1: 59–85.

Tagg, C. and A. Lyons (2018) Mobile messaging by migrant micro-entrepreneurs in contexts of superdiversity. In Creese, A. and A. Blackledge (eds) *The Routledge Handbook of Language and Superdiversity*. Abingdon: Routledge, pp. 312–328.

Tagg, C. and A. Lyons (2021) Polymedia repertoires of networked individuals: a day-in-the-life approach. *Pragmatics and Society* 12/5: 725–755.

Tagg, C. and M. Evans (2020) *Message and Medium: English Language Practices Across Old and New Media*. Berlin: De Gruyter Mouton.

Tagg, C. and P. Seargeant (2014) Audience design and language choice in the construction and maintenance of translocal communities on social network sites. In Seargeant, P. and C. Tagg (eds) *The Language of Social Media: Identity and Community on the Internet*. Basingstoke: Palgrave Macmillan, pp. 161–185.

Tagg, C. and R. Hu (2017) Sharing as a conversational turn in digital interaction. *Working Papers in Translanguaging and Translation* (WP29). Available: https://tlang.org.uk/working-papers/ (accessed 07/04/21).

Tagg, C., A. Lyons, R. Hu and F. Rock (2017) The ethics of digital ethnography in a team project. *Applied Linguistics Review* 8/2–3: 271–292.

Tagg, C., P. Seargeant and A. Aisha Brown (2017) *Taking Offence on Social Media: Communication and Conviviality on Facebook*. London: Palgrave.

Tagg, C., R. Hu, A. Lyons and J. Simpson (2016) Heritage and social media in superdiverse cities: personalised, networked and multimodal. *Working Papers in Translanguaging and Translation* (WP17). Available: https://tlang.org.uk/working-papers/ (accessed 07/04/21).

Takahashi, T. (2010) MySpace or Mixi? Japanese engagement with SNS (social networking sites) in the global age. *New Media and Society* 12/3: 453–75.

Takahashi, T. (2014) Youth, social media and connectivity in Japan. In Seargeant, P. and C. Tagg (eds) *The Language of Social Media: Identity and Community on the Internet*. London: Palgrave, pp. 186–207.

Tang, Y. and K.F. Hew (2019) Emoticon, emoji, and sticker use in computer-mediated communication: a review of theories and research findings. *International Journal of Communication* 13: 2457–2483.

Tannen, D. (1989) *Talking Voices: Repetition, Dialogue, and Imagery in Conversational Discourse*. Cambridge: Cambridge University Press.

Taylor, T.L. (2006) *Play between Worlds: Exploring Online Game Culture*. Cambridge, MA: MIT Press.

Taylor, A.S., and R. Harper (2002) Age-old practices in the 'New World': a study of gift giving between teenage mobile phone users. *Proceedings of the SIGCHI Conference on Human Factors in Computing Systems* 439–446. New York: ACM.

Tucker, L.R. (1998) The framing of Calvin Klein: a frame analysis of media discourse about the August 1995 Calvin Klein jeans advertising campaign. *Critical Studies in Mass Communication* 15: 141–157.

Thurlow, C. and M. Poff (2013) The language of text messaging. In Herring, S.C., D. Stein and T. Virtanen (eds) *Handbook of the Pragmatics of CMC*. Berlin and New York: Mouton de Gruyter.

Thurlow, C. with A. Brown (2003) Generation txt? The sociolinguistics of young people's text-messaging. *Discourse Analysis Online* 1/1.

Ting-Toomey, S. (1993) Communication resourcefulness: an identity-negotiation perspective. In R. Wiseman and J. Koester (eds) *Intercultural communication competence*. Newbury Park, CA. Sage, pp. 72–111.

Turkle, S. (1995) *Life on the Screen: Identity in the Age of the Internet*. New York: Simon and Schuster.

Tusting, K. and J. Maybin (2007) Linguistic ethnography and interdisciplinarity: opening the discussion. *Journal of Sociolinguistics* 11/5: 575–583.

Varis, P. (2016) Digital ethnography. In Georgakopoulou, A. and T. Spilioti (eds) *The Routledge Handbook of Language and Digital Communication*. London: Routledge, pp. 55–68.

Velghe, F. (2014) *'This is almost like writing': Mobile Phones, Learning and Literacy in a South African Township*. Unpublished PhD thesis. The Netherlands: Tilburg University.

Venema, R. and K. Lobinger (2020) Visual bonding and intimacy: a repertoire-oriented study of photo-sharing in close personal relationships. In Thurlow, C., C. Dürscheid and F. Diémoz (eds) *Visualising Digital Discourse: Interactional, Institutional and Ideological Perspectives*. Berlin: De Gruyter Mouton, pp. 171–185.

Wakeford, N. (2003) Internet cafés in London: the embedding of local culture in global communication: independent. *New Media & Society* 5/3: 379–399.

Wang (2016) More than words? The effect of line character sticker use on intimacy in the mobile communication environment. *Social Science Computer Review* 34/4: 456–478.

Welter, F. and M. Xheneti (2013) Reenacting contextual boundaries – entrepreneurial resourcefulness in challenging environments. In Corbett, A.C. and J.A. Katz (eds) *Entrepreneurial Resourcefulness: Competing with Constraints*. Bingley: Emerald Group, pp. 149–183.

Wessendorf, S. (2014) 'Being open, but sometimes closed'. Conviviality in a super-diverse London neighbourhood. *European Journal of Cultural Studies* 17/4: 392–405.

Williams, B. (2009) *Shimmering Literacies: Popular Culture and Reading and Writing Online*. New York: Peter Lang.

Zappavigna, M. (2012) *The Discourse of Twitter and Social Media*. London: Continuum.

Zhao, S. and M. Zappavigna (2018) Beyond the self: intersubjectivity and the social semiotic interpretation of the selfie. *New Media & Society* 20/5: 1735–1754.

Zhou, R., J. Hentschel and N. Kumar (2017) *Goodbye text, hello emoji: mobile communication on WeChat in China*. CHI 2017, May 6–11, Denver, CO, USA.

Index